SECOND EDITION

Google Apps Script

SO-BNT-248

James Ferreira

Beijing · Cambridge · Farnham · Köln · Sebastopol · Tokyo   O'REILLY®

Google Apps Script, Second Edition

by James Ferreira

Copyright © 2014 James Ferreira. All rights reserved.

Printed in the United States of America.

Published by O'Reilly Media, Inc., 1005 Gravenstein Highway North, Sebastopol, CA 95472.

O'Reilly books may be purchased for educational, business, or sales promotional use. Online editions are also available for most titles (*http://my.safaribooksonline.com*). For more information, contact our corporate/institutional sales department: 800-998-9938 or *corporate@oreilly.com*.

Editor: Mary Treseler	**Indexer:** Judy McConville
Production Editor: Nicole Shelby	**Cover Designer:** Randy Comer
Copyeditor: Becca Freed	**Interior Designer:** David Futato
Proofreader: Rachel Head	**Illustrator:** Rebecca Demarest

March 2014:   Second Edition

Revision History for the Second Edition:

2014-03-21:   First release

See *http://oreilly.com/catalog/errata.csp?isbn=9781491946183* for release details.

ISBN: 978-1-491-94618-3

[LSI]

Table of Contents

Preface. vii

Part I.   Understanding Google Apps Script

1. First Steps in Google Apps Script. 3
Google Apps Script Is…   3
What You Will Get from This Book   4
Getting Started   5
    Looking Around the Editor   6
Three Ways to Create a UI   10
    Hello Container-Bound Apps   11
    Hello Web App   16
    Hello, Google Sites   20
Web App Versus Container-Bound   22
Up and Walking   23

2. Setting Up Your Development Environment. 25
How to Debug and Test   26
    Handling Errors and Breaks   26
    Break and Report   27
Production Error Logging   28
    Logging the Backend   28
    Logging HTML Frontends   29
Wrapping Up   32

3. Building an Interface. 33
What's in a UI?   33
It Starts with doGet   33
Contact Me   35

Getting Started   35

4. Adding Actions. 41
   Handling User Actions   41
   Anatomy of a Handler   41
   The Concept of the Callback   43
   Functions Are Where the Action Happens   46
   Storing the Values   46
      Storing in a Spreadsheet   47
      Setting Up the Spreadsheet   47
      Setting Up the Data   49

Part II.   Building Enterprise Applications

5. Dynamic Details: A Sites App Using HTML, CSS, and jQuery. 53
   Fighting Clutter   53
   What You Will Learn   55
   Supplies   55
   Application Overview   55
   Image File Repository   55
      Setting Up the Database   56
      Loading the Database   57
   Creating Pages from a Spreadsheet   59
      Using the Public Google Apps Script Objects Class   59
      Using JavaScript Objects   60
      Installing an Open Source Library   60
      Creating Pages and Filling the Spreadsheet   62
   Creating the Products UI   67
      Displaying Products   68
      Creating the Products Table   70
      Adding Action   72
      Mousing Around   73
   Delivering the Application   77
   Final Code   78

6. Automate Your Forms and Templates: A Web App for Drive. 81
   What You Will Learn   82
   Supplies   82
   Application Overview   82
   Setting Up the Template   82
   Building the Script   84

UI Setup   85
Selecting the Template   87
Getting the Keys   89
Generating the Form   90
Submitting the Completed Form   92
Copying the Template and Adding Responses   92
Final Code   94

7. Collecting Data: A UiApp-Style Web App. **99**
The Installed App Has Died   99
What You Will Learn   100
Supplies   100
Application Overview   100
Setting Up   102
Building the Foundation   103
  Main Panel   103
  Headers Grid   104
  Branding   104
  Search Component   105
  Navigation Component   107
  Content Area   108
  Search View   109
  Creating the Data Store   111
Configuring Fusion Tables Access   112
  Getting Data from a Fusion Table   114
  Loading the Data in the UI   115
  Adding Client-Side Handlers   118
Viewing a Record   119
  Fetching the Correct Record   119
  Custom Formatting   122
  Formatting a listBox   123
Editing a Record   125
Saving Changes   127
Inserting a New Record   128
Deleting a Record   131
Full Code   132

8. Document Workflows. **141**
Building a Modern Email Workflow   142
What You Will Learn   142
Supplies   142
Application Overview   142

Creating the Menus   143
Loading the Sidebar   145
Starting the Workflow   147
    Start Workflow HTML   147
    Start Workflow JavaScript   150
    Using ScriptDB   151
    Adding Approvers   152
    Loading the Approvers   153
    Removing Approvers   155
    Pressing Start   156
Recording Approvals   158
Approval Status   162
Audit History   166
Resetting Everything   168
Deploying Using Add-ons   171
Finishing Up   171
Full Code   171

9. Mashup.   183
Directing Email Using Google Forms   183
Charts in Sites   187
    FinanceApp Chart   187
    Chart from a Spreadsheet   191

Index.   195

Preface

If you are reading this book, there is a good chance you have heard of Google and its powerful office productivity suite, Google Apps. Google offers search, email, word processing, and hundreds of other cloud applications and services that are available to individuals but can scale all the way up to serve massive corporations and governments. As one of Google's most popular services, Google Apps offers some of the best online office products available; they're an excellent example of web-based applications that outperform legacy desktop software.

This book is about Google Apps Script, which is a service that runs from Google Apps, like Sites and Documents. Google Apps Script is extremely powerful when automating many of the tasks required by day-to-day spreadsheet operations, but it also scales up to provide a complete application platform. If you are coming from a Microsoft Office environment, you can think of it as the macros for Google Docs, but unlike simple macros in MS Office, Google Apps Script has a mature online editor with all the features one would expect in a development platform. Unleash Google Script's user interface capability and you can create entire data-driven websites and applications that run across most modern browsers, including mobile ones.

In addition to the integrated development environment (IDE), Google Apps Script comes with a manager for organizing scripts, built-in debugging, automatic code completion, timed event triggers, and automated revisioning, to name a few features. What really caught this author's attention was that everything is web-based. There is no need to download and configure a code editor or transport development files from computer to computer, wasting time resynchronizing files and reconnecting libraries. Simply sign into your Google account and start creating. Google Apps Scripts are written in JavaScript, so there is no need to compile the code, making application development very fast.

With its own set of libraries, Google Apps Script can interact with most of the services provided by Google, making it the "Swiss Army knife" behind the main products. Other application-building methods for accessing Google products, such as App Engine and the gData APIs (offered in many different languages), all require a place for you to develop and deploy your code. With Google Apps Script, you are building the code into the existing Google platform, and that provides a robust experience where your products inherit Google's legendary 99.9 percent availability. Because there is no need to have anything more than a basic Internet-connected browser, development on this platform is something anyone can get started with, without any up-front expense. Google Apps Script is not locked inside Google, where it can only talk to Google servers; rather, it can communicate through JDBC, JSON, and SOAP, and it has a `urlFetch` method, making it very versatile when communicating across the Web.

At Google I/O 2012 a new feature called HTML Service was unveiled, giving Google Apps Script programmers the ability to build custom user interfaces that can run inside a spreadsheet window as a Google gadget or completely independently in a browser. Talk about earth-shattering: a cloud programing platform that can access just about any web-based service and has the ability to create AJAX-style web pages? That is noteworthy. To date, Google Apps Script is the only way to gain full access to Gmail at the message level, and more services are added every year.

This book will focus on teaching you how to build powerful web applications using Google Apps Script. It is laid out in sections that explain how the different parts of Google Apps Script work and puts all these together in a series of fully functional applications that you can put to work right away.

Who Should Read This Book

This book is perfect for anyone who wants to extend what can be done with Google Apps but is not ready to dive into the complicated world of the Google Web Toolkit and Java APIs. You don't have to be a webmaster or programmer to grasp the concepts in this book. Google Apps Script takes care of server configuration, gives you a place to save your projects, and allows you to start developing immediately. This book is approachable by anyone with basic coding skills and a fundamental understanding of JavaScript. If you have never used JavaScript, I recommend having a copy of *Head First JavaScript* (O'Reilly) close at hand to help you through concepts like variables, arrays, and objects. All the application examples have highly detailed explanations, so if you are a Google Apps power user, you should not have difficulty grasping the content in this book and writing incredible applications using Google Apps Script.

What You Will Need

You will need a web browser (I recommend Chrome) and any type of Google account. That's it! Google Apps Script is a completely web-based solution that is free and ready for you to start programming today.

Conventions Used in This Book

The following typographical conventions are used in this book:

Italic

> Indicates new terms, URLs, email addresses, and file extensions.

`Constant width`

> Used for program listings, as well as within paragraphs to refer to program elements such as variable or function names, databases, data types, environment variables, statements, and keywords.

`Constant width bold`

> Shows commands or other text that should be typed literally by the user.

`Constant width italic`

> Shows text that should be replaced with user-supplied values or by values determined by context.

 This element signifies a tip or suggestion.

 This element signifies a general note.

 This element indicates a warning or caution.

Using Code Examples

At the end of each chapter you will find the full code used to create that chapter's project. In addition, you may access all the files used to create this book in the book's Drive folder (*http://goo.gl/zqy3VQ*).

This book is here to help you get your job done. In general, if example code is offered with this book, you may use it in your programs and documentation. You do not need to contact us for permission unless you're reproducing a significant portion of the code.

For example, writing a program that uses several chunks of code from this book does not require permission. Selling or distributing a CD-ROM of examples from O'Reilly books does require permission. Answering a question by citing this book and quoting example code does not require permission. Incorporating a significant amount of example code from this book into your product's documentation does require permission.

We appreciate, but do not require, attribution. An attribution usually includes the title, author, publisher, and ISBN. For example: "*Google Apps Script* by James Ferreira (O'Reilly). Copyright 2014 James Ferreira, 978-1-491-94618-3."

If you feel your use of code examples falls outside fair use or the permission given above, feel free to contact us at *permissions@oreilly.com*.

Safari® Books Online

 Safari Books Online is an on-demand digital library that delivers expert content in both book and video form from the world's leading authors in technology and business.

Technology professionals, software developers, web designers, and business and creative professionals use Safari Books Online as their primary resource for research, problem solving, learning, and certification training.

Safari Books Online offers a range of product mixes and pricing programs for organizations, government agencies, and individuals. Subscribers have access to thousands of books, training videos, and prepublication manuscripts in one fully searchable database from publishers like O'Reilly Media, Prentice Hall Professional, Addison-Wesley Professional, Microsoft Press, Sams, Que, Peachpit Press, Focal Press, Cisco Press, John Wiley & Sons, Syngress, Morgan Kaufmann, IBM Redbooks, Packt, Adobe Press, FT Press, Apress, Manning, New Riders, McGraw-Hill, Jones & Bartlett, Course Technology, and dozens more. For more information about Safari Books Online, please visit us online.

How to Contact Us

Please address comments and questions concerning this book to the publisher:

O'Reilly Media, Inc.
1005 Gravenstein Highway North
Sebastopol, CA 95472
800-998-9938 (in the United States or Canada)
707-829-0515 (international or local)
707-829-0104 (fax)

We have a web page for this book, where we list errata, examples, and any additional information. You can access this page at *http://oreil.ly/google-script*.

To comment or ask technical questions about this book, send email to *bookques tions@oreilly.com*.

For more information about our books, courses, conferences, and news, see our website at *http://www.oreilly.com*.

Find us on Facebook: *http://facebook.com/oreilly*

Follow us on Twitter: *http://twitter.com/oreillymedia*

Watch us on YouTube: *http://www.youtube.com/oreillymedia*

Understanding Google Apps Script

PART I
Understanding Google App Script

First Steps in Google Apps Script

What is Google Apps Script and why should you use it to build applications? Simply put, Google Apps Script is an easy way to figuratively glue Google and other web services together to form one powerful, interactive web application. Just ahead, you'll get a more in-depth explanation of Google Apps Script and how to use it to enhance existing Google Apps. You will also learn the basics of building an application. This first chapter should get your feet firmly planted on the ground floor of the Google Apps Script development platform and demystify its usage.

Google Apps Script Is...

Google Apps Script is a coding and application development platform built into Google Apps, enabling you to add functionality to spreadsheets, Gmail, Sites, and other services from Google. For example, if your spreadsheet needs a menu item in the toolbar for creating a pivot table, you can write a Google Apps Script that adds it to the menu and performs the task. Google Apps Scripts can be created as standalone files in Drive, inside a document or spreadsheet (these are known as *container-bound*), or in a Google Site.

This book will focus extensively on the concept of using Google Apps Script to build applications that present themselves as web services running independently of other interfaces. You will learn how to use Google Apps Script to build apps that run from a spreadsheet, in a browser window, or within a Google Site; from the user's perspective, they will appear to be complete applications such as you might expect when using a web service like Picasa or Gmail.

There are some real advantages to having your scripts (i.e., applications) stored in one of the Google Apps services. Primarily, security is already built in, meaning you do not need to worry about implementing that component in your application as you would if it were running on a legacy web server needing patches and constant monitoring for malicious attacks. As part of Google Apps, Google Apps Script also offers you the same collaborative development abilities that are part of the Apps suite. What is truly exciting about Google Apps Script is that it is a 100 percent web development environment that requires no transferring of files from computer to computer, backups, revision control, uploads to a production server, updating of development software, or many of the other tedious aspects of development that get in the way of actually writing applications. These parts are all built in, allowing you to focus on creating products for your business, school or club, or anything else that needs to run on the Web.

If you are an advanced developer coming from Google App Engine, don't worry; there is a plug-in for Eclipse that will allow you to work on the files locally, and they will automatically be pushed up to Google.

There are three ways to create user interfaces (UIs) in Google Apps Script: with the older UiApp Service, as gadgets for Google Sites, and using the HTML Service. The UiApp Service, which stands for User Interface App, was released in early 2010 as a way to allow developers to collect user input that could be sent back to a script for processing. UiApp uses the Google Web Toolkit (GWT) widget set as the framework for building an interface. Widgets allow you to create things like text boxes and submit buttons, as well as more complex items like flex tables and listboxes. Everything you see in a Google Apps Script UI is a widget cleverly arranged within a frame in the page. The only other elements—panels—are the containers that hold all your widgets…and that is truly all there is to the visual part of a Google Apps Script UI. If you are familiar with GWT, you will be right at home creating UIs in Google Apps Script using UiApp.

At the 2013 Google I/O, Google Apps Script received a major update to the way UIs are presented. The new HTML Service uses standard HTML, Cascading Style Sheets (CSS), and JavaScript to display pages. This means you don't need to worry about learning the intricacies of GWT, and you can use many existing JavaScript libraries, like jQuery (*http://jquery.com/*). As of this writing Google is using Caja (*https://develop ers.google.com/caja/*), which will limit some of the functionality you might get out of an advanced library like Bootstrap (*http://getbootstrap.com/*), so beware.

Google has not officially deprecated UiApp, but it will not be receiving much in the way of updates in the future. Google strongly recommends converting to the HTML Service.

What You Will Get from This Book

By the time you get to the back cover of this book, you will have learned all the necessary elements that go into building web applications using Google Apps Script. With this knowledge under your belt, you will be able to create your own applications and take full advantage of your Google-hosted services. Your apps will have the ability to recognize and authenticate users and carry out tasks such as displaying custom data from a spreadsheet, data entry, sending emails, and so much more. Have a look at Part II to see the kinds of applications we will be building and let your imagination flow.

Getting Started

Enough preamble—let's dig in!

For the most part, we will be building our scripts in the Google Drive Service. To get started with the examples in this chapter load up Google Drive (*http://drive.google.com*). From here, click the "Create" button and choose "Script." If you don't have the Script App, it can be installed by clicking the "Connect more apps" button at the bottom of the "Create" menu and searching for "Apps Script." You can also get started by simply going to the Google Apps Script start page (*http://www.google.com/script/start*) and clicking the "Start Scripting" button (Figure 1-1).

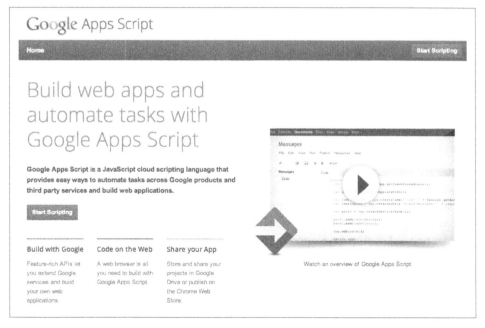

Figure 1-1. All scripts are saved in your Google Drive

The Google Script Editor will open as a new window. It gives you the option to create your project from a template as well as to access some useful tutorials (see Figure 1-2).

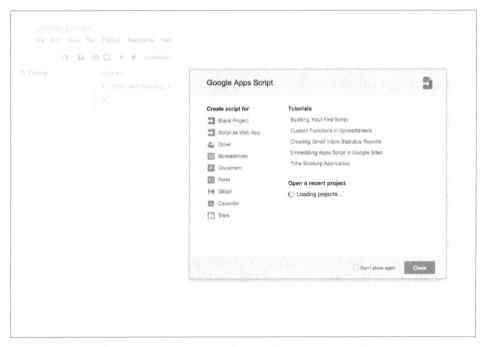

Figure 1-2. Templates are working examples to help you get started

Looking Around the Editor

Before writing your first script, let's take a look at some of the features in the Google Script Editor. First off you will notice that it looks much like what you already know from Google Docs.

Under the File menu are the typical Save, Delete, Rename, New, etc. (Figure 1-3). And as with many of the other Google Apps services, Google Apps Script has a Manage Versions feature that will allow you to turn back the clock to a point when your code *was* working. Not that we ever need such features… But seriously, we often go down the wrong road during development, and revisions can save you hours of trying to get back to a known good point. When launched, a pop-up Revisions box will show what the code looked like in the version you selected.

File　Edit　View　Run　Publish　Resources　Help

New

Open...　⌘O

See revision history　⌘⌥⌘G

Rename...

Delete...

Make a copy...

Save　⌘S

Save all　⌘⇧S

Manage versions...　EXPERIMENTAL!

Upgrade authorization experience...

Project properties

Build a user interface...　DEPRECATED!

Figure 1-3. Saving is not automatic

When you have the Revisions box open, you can select and copy parts of the code. This is handy when you may have gone down two different paths and want to roll back one part without losing the other.

In the File menu there are some very important options. *Project properties* make it possible to store a limited amount of information in key/value pairs for use by your script at runtime. Properties can be edited in the box that pops up after clicking the Properties option in the File menu, or by using the Properties Service right in your code. Many of the apps in this book will need to sign into non-Google services, and Script Properties is a great place to store something like a password.

The "Manage versions" selection is used for applications you deploy as web apps or libraries and gives you a way to control the version your users are accessing. This feature allows you to update your existing production application without disturbing your users. Once you are ready to move everyone to the latest version, you simply change the version.

There's nothing very exciting in the Edit menu, other than "Find and replace" (Figure 1-4). The replace functionality is a good way to globally change the name of a variable. Figure 1-4

Figure 1-4. The Edit menu

On the View menu, shown in Figure 1-5, there are some important options: "execution," "transcript," and "logs." When a script is run from the editor or by you as the user from a web interface or container, the execution transcript will list each command as it is run. Using the execution transcript, you can see the order that the code is executed in, which is helpful in debugging. Logs are used along with the Logger Service and allow the writing of information and other notes as a way to track information. This was particularly useful before the Debugger was added and is a big help when testing code. I want to reiterate that these features only work from the Script Editor and will not be of much use debugging in the UiApp and HTML Services when your application is run from the browser. Don't worry, there is a whole section in this book to help you debug like a pro.

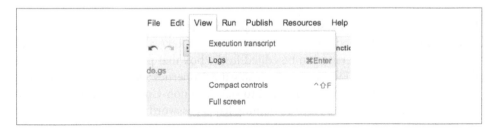

Figure 1-5. The View menu

Learn by doing is how I figure this stuff out, so let's jump in and give the Logger a try. Add the following line of code into the Script Editor:

```
function myFunction(){
  Logger.log('A test of the Log');
}
```

Click Run (you might be asked to name your file), and then check the Logs under the View menu (Figure 1-6).

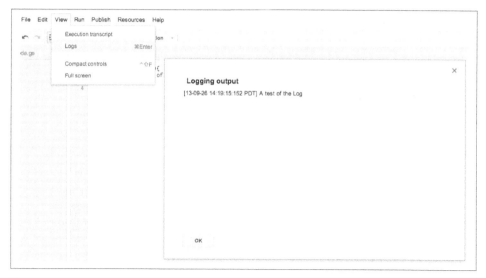

Figure 1-6. Log output

The Publish menu is where you will find the "Deploy as web app" option, which makes displaying a UI possible. This is also the place for distributing your application on the Google Chrome Web Store. We will be covering these features in great detail later in the book.

The Resources menu provides access to *triggers* (see Figure 1-7), which are the automation component that can run a script at specified times or after certain events, like upon the submission of a form or when the spreadsheet is edited. Triggers are very useful for tasks such as backing up information at 1 a.m., so you get credit for working hard while fast asleep. Also in the Resources menu you will find *libraries*. These are scripts that are written by other developers and can be added using the script's special key, found under File→"Project properties." A library is typically a set of functions that extend or fill gaps in the platform. For example, you may want to access YouTube, but until December 2013, Google Apps Script did not have a YouTube Service. Before the Google connector was available, someone (hint: your author) wrote and offered a You-Tube App Library (*http://bit.ly/youtube-ex*) to help developers easily work with the YouTube API, without having to figure out the details of parsing XML necessary when using Google APIs directly.

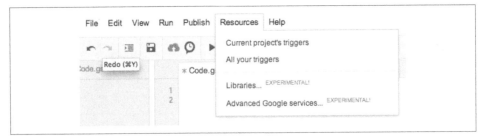

Figure 1-7. The Resources menu

 You don't need to be an important public official to have your own library in Google Apps Script. In fact, anyone can create a library— and the more developers provide excellent libraries, the better Google Apps Script will be. Have a look at the Google Apps Script Examples page (*http://bit.ly/useful-lib*) for several helpful libraries.

That's about it for the menus. Figure 1-8 shows a few buttons that explain themselves and make for easier access to the most commonly used features.

Figure 1-8. Buttons make for easy access to common tasks

The "Debug" button (the bug) next to the "Run" button (the arrow) will bring up a window at the bottom of the code window and show the values of your code as it is executed. It has features for setting breakpoints and stepping in and over parts of code, and it will make developing non-UI parts of your code much easier. The user documentation on the Google Apps Script website goes into detail on using the Debugger (*http://bit.ly/gas-overview*).

Three Ways to Create a UI

There are three ways to create and display a user interface (UI) in Google Apps Script. The first way is in a spreadsheet, as a pop-up window or sidebar; the second, as a web page; and the third as a gadget in a Google Sites page.

As you work through this chapter, please note that some of the code in each type of UI is the same and will only be described once, as it is first introduced. It would be a good idea to go through all the different UI types to avoid any confusion and to gain an understanding of when and why a certain UI type would work better for your application.

Hello Container-Bound Apps

Now that you know your way around the Script Editor, it is time to write your first script. The first type of UI is called *container-bound* because it is going to display as a pop-up window or sidebar in your spreadsheet or document. The term "container-bound" comes from requiring a spreadsheet or document to display the UI, but this does not mean that any certain type of UI is more or less integrated than another. A script contained in a document can display a web page or pop-up, and scripts created in Drive can access spreadsheets. I am simply giving you a reference for what we are discussing because the code to display each type differs slightly.

The UiApp Service

From a spreadsheet, click Tools and select "Script editor." The Script Editor will open. Dismiss the getting started pop-up, delete all of the example code, and add the following code:

```
function helloWorldUiApp() {
  var ss = SpreadsheetApp.getActiveSpreadsheet();
  var app = UiApp.createApplication().setTitle(<Your Title>);
  app.add(app.createLabel('Hello World'));
  //TODO add your code here
  ss.show(app);
}
```

Click "Save," and name your project "Hello World Container Bound" (see Figure 1-9).

Figure 1-9. Naming your project

Now click "Run." We are using SpreadsheetApp, so the first thing you will see is a request for you to authorize the app (Figure 1-10).

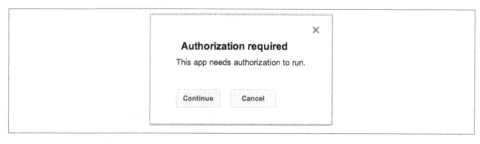

Figure 1-10. Authorization required

Next, you will see another screen telling you which parts of Google your app would like to access. If you agree to let your app access your spreadsheet, click Accept (Figure 1-11). Remember, when you build apps that other people use, they will also see this screen.

Figure 1-11. Granting access

Google is always working to make the authorization process better, so in the future you may not need to go through as many screens asking you the same questions.

A status message will appear at the top of the editor letting you know the script is being run (Figure 1-12).

Figure 1-12. Script is running

Once the run operation completes, switch your browser window to the spreadsheet, and you will see a pop-up window that says "Hello World" (Figure 1-13).

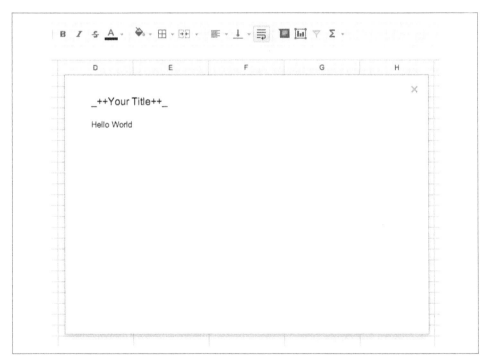

Figure 1-13. "Hello World" spreadsheet

The HTML Service

If you remember, there was a warning a few pages back that said the UiApp Service is not the direction Google is going in. Well, let's now learn the new way we build UIs in Google Apps Script. The rest of the book will focus mainly on the HTML Service, so please take the time here to understand the components and how they work together.

We could redo the UiApp spreadsheet example from before, but I don't want you to get bored. I also want to show you one of the other new features: the *sidebar* in Docs. This example will require a Google Doc, so go ahead and create a new doc in Drive. Next, click "Tools" and select "Script editor."

Replace the default code with the following:

```
function helloWorldHtmlService() {
  var ui = DocumentApp.getUi();
  var html = HtmlService.createTemplateFromFile('sideBar').evaluate()
      .setTitle('Sidebar Example').setWidth(300)
      .setSandboxMode(HtmlService.SandboxMode.NATIVE);
  ui.showSidebar(html);
}
```

The HTML Service is, just as it says, built using HTML. Normally when you are working in Google Apps Script you are using *.gs* (Google Script) file types to write your code. Now you can also write standard HTML files that use the common things you would find on any modern web page, like jQuery and CSS. To create an HTML file, click File and select New, then "Html file" (see Figure 1-14). You will be asked to name your file. Name it "sideBar," as this is the file we are referring to in the *code.gs* file.

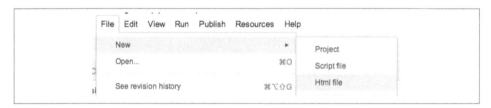

Figure 1-14. Creating an HTML file

For this example we will use the basic structure of a web page, including head and body tags. Copy the following code into the new *sideBar.html* file:

```
<html>
  <head>
  </head>
  <body>
    <div>Hello World</div>
  </body>
</html>
```

The result is two files of the types *.gs* and *.html* (Figure 1-15).

Figure 1-15. Two files

Click the "Save" button and switch back to the *code.gs* file by clicking its tab. Now run `helloWorldHtmlService`. Once the script completes, switch to the Document tab in your web browser to see the new sidebar open, as shown in Figure 1-16.

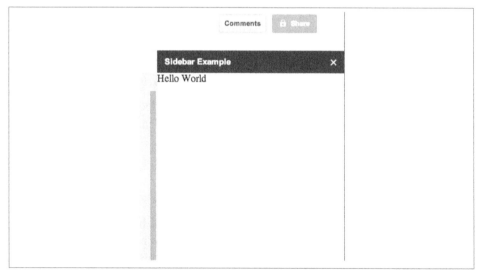

Figure 1-16. The amazing sidebar

Diving into the HTML Service code

Now that you see how it works, let's break down the components so you can understand them. In the *code.gs* file we have used the custom function `helloWorldHtmlService` to wrap the code in; you can name these functions whatever you like within the JavaScript naming rules. Several other functions have names that are specific to Google Apps Script. I want to stop for a second to mention `doGet`, which is used to load web apps after you publish them. More on that later.

 The function names `doGet`, `doPost`, `onEdit`, `onInstall`, and `onOp en` are special, reserved names and should not be used as names of any custom functions of yours that do not perform these specific operations.

Next we will need to get the document, so we can use the DocumentApp Service (*http://bit.ly/docu-service*) to work with the sidebar or dialog windows:

```
var ui = DocumentApp.getUi();+ We use the method +getUi
```

The DocumentApp UI object is saved in the variable `ui` so we can add stuff to it.

The next long line is where we load up the HTML file *sideBar.html*. I have added several methods to set the width, give it a title at the top of the page, and force `SandboxMode`, which will make the UI load faster:

```
var html = HtmlService.createTemplateFromFile('sideBar').evaluate()
    .setTitle('Sidebar Example').setWidth(300)
    .setSandboxMode(HtmlService.SandboxMode.NATIVE);
```

The HTML Service (*http://bit.ly/html-service*) has two different methods of displaying the content from your HTML file, which we cover in "It Starts with doGet" on page 33.

The last part is where we add the rendered HTML to the document UI that we stored earlier in the `ui` variable. The `showSidebar` method also opens the sidebar in the document:

```
ui.showSidebar(html);
```

Hello Web App

The second type of UI application is referred to as a *web app* because the UI is accessed from a special URL hosted in Google's cloud. There is no need for a spreadsheet or document container to use the web app, but you can build this type of UI in a container or in any of the Google services where the Script Editor is available. The URL can be made public, allowing DNS mapping to your domain; for example, *http://Your_Great_App.domain.com*.

Time to build your first web app!

Go to Google Drive and click the "Create" button. In the Create menu click the "Script" icon (Figure 1-17).

Figure 1-17. The Create menu

 You may not see the Script icon in your Create menu. In this case, click the "Connect more apps" button at the bottom of the menu and add it.

After the Script Editor opens, replace the myFunction code with:

```
function doGet() {
  var html = HtmlService.createTemplateFromFile('index').evaluate()
      .setTitle('Web App').setSandboxMode(HtmlService.SandboxMode.NATIVE);
  return html;
}
```

The first difference from the container version is that we must have a doGet function for Google to grab when the special Google URL for our app is loaded in a browser. This is analogous to the entry point you might use in GWT. doGet is the starting point for loading visible elements in the web app UI.

Now click "File" and select "New," then "Html file." You will be asked to name your file. Call the file "index" and insert the following code:

```
<html>
  <head>
  </head>
```

```
  <body>
    <div>Hello Web App</div>
  </body>
</html>
```

Now save both files, and let's get ready to publish.

Publishing options

In the Script Editor, click Publish and select "Deploy as web app." The "Deploy as web app" dialog opens (Figure 1-18).

Figure 1-18. The "Deploy as web app" dialog

Because this is the first time you have published this script, you will see a "Product version" box. You don't need to type anything in the box, but you do need to click the "Save New Version" button to set the first version. The next time you come back to this menu, this section will be a drop-down selection.

 The next time you publish this app, you will need to save a new version by going to File and clicking "Manage versions." Versioning will be covered in Chapter 3.

There are a few important choices here. "Execute the app as" allows you to select how the app runs: as you or as the person running the app. You'll have to weigh the options to decide which is best. If you're building apps that you will distribute to others to run for enhancing their Google Apps, then you will want your app to run as them and access their data. On the other hand, you might want the users to do something like enter values on your spreadsheet from a form UI but not have access to the spreadsheet itself. When the app runs as you, it accesses your data. Unforunately, it's one way or the other, and if your app needs access to both your information and the user's… well, it gets a bit more complex. Don't worry—we will cover how to handle this later in the book.

For this example you can leave the execution setting as yourself.

 The "yada yada" Google refers to is a serious warning. When you build a standalone application, it will run as you and it will have access to anything you have given it permission to see. For example, be careful not to publish the contents of your email inbox to everyone on the Web.

Now that you know how the app will run, you will need to set who can use it. These settings are similar to what you expect to see in most Google services. Note that your choice applies to the web app, *not* the script, which is set from the blue button in the Script Editor. The setting "Anyone, even anonymous" will allow your app to run without the user signing into a Google account. If your app is just showing text or running as you this may be a good choice, but it is not going to go well for the user if your app accesses her Google Drive. Be careful to think through these two settings and what your app needs to do; but don't worry, you can change them at any time.

Leave the selection set to "Only myself" and click the "Deploy" button. Now for the drumroll: a new window pops up (Figure 1-19).

Figure 1-19. Getting the current web app URL

This box contains the *current web app URL*, which will be where you can send all your friends to see the great things you're learning. This is what we refer to as the *production link*, because it will always be running the version you set in the previous window. If you look just below the box you will see a "latest code" link, which opens a URL that ends in */dev*. This is the development version and reflects the code as it is in the editor every time you save. You will use this link a lot, because saving a new version and republishing every time you made a change would drive you nuts!

This special URL is for the page where the app is being hosted on Google's servers. If you forget it, simply open the Publish dialog and copy it again. Click OK and open a new tab in your browser. Paste the URL into the address bar and load the page. You should now see your app displaying the text from the HTML you created earlier (Figure 1-20).

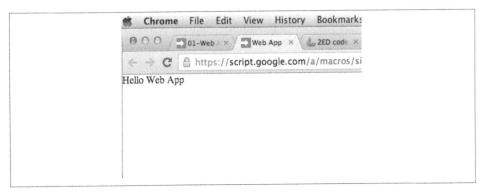

Figure 1-20. First HTML Service UI

Congratulations! You have just created your first Google Apps Script UI web app. Not much of an "app" yet, but as you can see, it takes very little effort to get an application pushed out to a web interface. You might feel tht you have missed a few steps here, which can be a good thing. For starters, you did not need to set up Apache, or figure out how to FTP to a web server somewhere to upload files. For that matter, you didn't need to purchase and install a Web server or buy a domain name. Google Apps Script lets you write your application entirely on the web and then takes care of the rest of the details. I don't want to say it gets easier from here, but this is the foundation. After this, the functionality of providing a service has more to do with adding div tags and filling them with data; there is no more that needs to be done to create the UI service or web page. Maintenance, access, and version tracking are integrated, which means you can focus on the code.

Hello, Google Sites

To this point, we've been using Google Docs to work with the Script Editor and create UIs. However, the editor is also available in the Google Sites service, allowing UI scripts to be inserted as gadgets appearing on the pages in your sites. This is tremendously exciting for Google Sites users because it means having the ability to create complex interactions that would normally require code hosted on a server somewhere else. For example, a business could feature products with color options that the user can change to see a different look, an HR department application might allow training signup pages that bring back live calendar results, or a school could host an educational game for students. These are just a few examples, but the options are virtually limitless. Chapter 5 is about making gadgets for Google Sites in Google Apps Script; for now let's focus on the basics.

First you are going to need a Google Site (*http://sites.google.com*), then go and click that red "Create" button on the left side. Now name your site and click once more on the "Create" button. Voilà, you have a site.

Google Apps Script UIs run as gadgets in Google Sites, and you can even write and manage the code from within the site's management console. In your site's page, click on More and select "Manage site." In the left-side menu, click "Apps Scripts" to open the Script Manager, as seen in Figure 1-21.

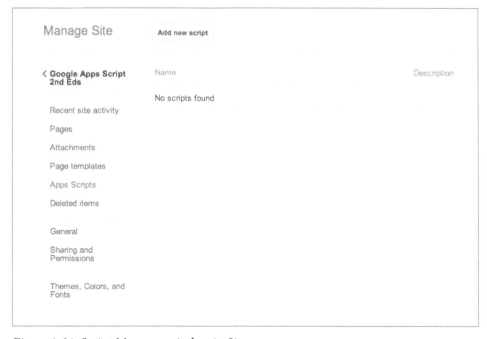

Figure 1-21. Script Manager window in Sites

Clicking the "Add new script" button opens the Script Editor you have seen all along. Go ahead and name your script "Script Gadget," then paste in the following code:

```
function doGet() {
  var html = HtmlService.createHtmlOutput('<h2>Hello World</h2>');
  return html;
}
```

Go through the deployment process described in "Publishing options" on page 18, and you'll be ready to add the gadget to the home page.

Go over to your Sites page and click the "Edit Page" button. Now, from the Insert menu choose "Apps Script" to get the script chooser menu (Figure 1-22).

Figure 1-22. Selecting a script

Click your "Script Gadget" file and then the "Select" button. There are some options next, but you can pretty much skip through three "Save" buttons to get back out to your home page. After a few seconds your UI will display.

You can also use any published UI as the URL for the gadget by using the box at the bottom of the Insert window.

Web App Versus Container-Bound

One of the most exciting features of the HTML Service is that it can run all by itself without the need of a container. This is accomplished by publishing the script, which creates an access point through a special Google URL. There are several options when publishing, such as restricting access to just you or opening up the app so anyone visiting the URL can run it. Publishing does not, however, allow visitors access to your code; that is controlled by the sharing settings in the Script Editor or container if publishing from there. This means you can create your application and the code will stay safely secured.

 One important thing to remember is that a script running as a published web service can run as *you* and will have access to the services to which you have granted access. Therefore, if your script lists all the emails in your Gmail Inbox and you make it public, anyone visiting the URL will see your Inbox. Settings are also available to make your script run as the user of the app. Just make sure you have the right settings before publishing.

Running the script as your account can be a benefit because you can set the spreadsheet sharing to limit access and then control what data a UI viewer sees while still allowing input into the spreadsheet. There will be more on this concept later when we start putting together real-world apps in Part II.

One limitation to having the script run as you, the creator, is that you will not be able to directly access a user's account from the built-in classes. For example, if your application needs to access the user's Google Contacts, it will not work that way. You don't have that user-to-user access in Google Apps, so it does not work in Google Apps Script either. Later in the book we will cover how to handle this problem using multiple scripts that talk to each other.

While I present these differences between the styles as hurdles, there are some very good reasons to have access restricted in this way. Fortunately, these security features don't limit us in building apps, but they add certain complexities that need to be considered.

Up and Walking

Here we are at the end of Chapter 1, and a lot of ground has been covered. We started with a description of where to find the Google Script Editor and what one might use it for, then progressed on to creating a new script. After that, you learned how to make your UI appear integrated into a Google Sheet, next a sidebar in a Google Doc, and lastly as an independent web page. Wow, that's a bunch of new stuff, but you should now have your feet under you and be able to find your way around the Google Apps Script service.

In Chapter 2, you will continue mastering Google Apps Script by learning about helpful ways to arrange your development environment and how to debug UI code.

Setting Up Your Development Environment

When developing a UI in Google Apps Script, you will often load the UI in a browser to see how code is rendered on the page. Among the several ways of displaying the UI during development, it is best to use the web app page and the "latest code" link described in "Publishing options" on page 18. The reason is that each time a change is made in the script, proofing that change only requires saving your script and reloading the page showing the development version of your app (or the "dev page").

The Script Editor has a built-in debugger that can help when you are working up the processing elements. For example, say you would like to retrieve some data from a SOAP service and parse the XML. The debugger will allow you to set breakpoints so you can step through the code and review values throughout the process.

Once you start using interactive elements in the UI, such as a click handler, you will not be able to use the debugger. This is because the frontend of the UI is loaded into the browser and is therefore independent of the Script Editor. Later in this chapter, we will introduce an error-catching method that will help you find problems in your code.

Most developers like to have an arrangement of code, live view, and console output like what's available in the Eclipse IDE. Figure 2-1 shows a layout of three browser windows that effectively creates an IDE look for Google Apps Script.

To create this setup, open a new window for the Script Editor, a spreadsheet to be used for error checking (see "Production Error Logging" on page 28), and the web app page. Now move and size them. You can get some more space by hiding toolbars that you don't need. When working with the HTML Service it will also be useful to open the JavaScript Console, which can be found in the Tools menu using Google Chrome.

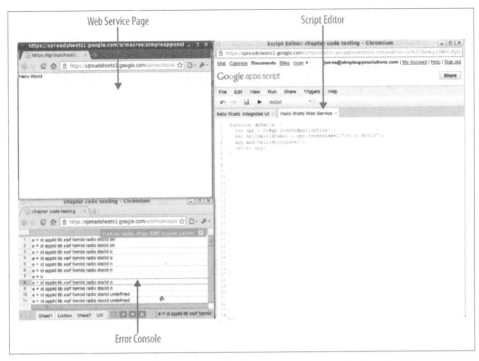

Web Service Page

Script Editor

Error Console

Figure 2-1. Arranging windows on your desktop can save time during development

How to Debug and Test

Each time you save a script, Google will run through the code and make sure there are no syntax errors. That does not mean the Script Editor will tell you if a variable is not defined or a web service could not be reached. It will tell you that you forgot a closing bracket or added an extra quote. This error checking is displayed at the top of the page in red with the error and line number where the issue occurs. When you run the script from the editor, the same notification will show runtime errors such as undefined variables.

Web apps must run on the client side in a browser window, spreadsheet, or gadget, which means that runtime errors can't be shown in the Script Editor. Next we will look at three ways of displaying errors for development and production.

Handling Errors and Breaks

Like most object-oriented programing languages, Google Apps Script uses the `try/catch` statement to work with errors at runtime. It is important to know that the browser will return errors as well; however, one can get more detail using `try/catch`.

Let's see this in practice: make a copy of the script you made in "Hello Web App" on page 16, rename it "Errors," and then publish the UI as explained in Chapter 1.

Copy and paste the following buggy code into your "Errors" script's *index.html* file:

```
function doGet() {
  var html = HtmlService.createTemplateFromFile('index').evaluate()
      .setTitle('Web App').setSandboxMode(HtmlService.SandboxMode.NATIVE);
      var x=t;
  return html;
}
```

Now reload the UI page and note the error: `ReferenceError: "t" is not defined`. Not much of a problem in our six lines of code to see where the problem is, but what if our code was 5,000 lines long?

Let's try that again using a `try/catch` statement and a UI element to display it:

```
function doGet() {
  try{
    var html = HtmlService.createTemplateFromFile('index').evaluate()
        .setTitle('Web App').setSandboxMode(HtmlService.SandboxMode NATIVE);
    var x=t;
  }catch(e){
    html.setContent(e.name + ' on line: ' + e.lineNumber + ' -> ' +
                    e.message);
  }
  return html;
}
```

Reload the UI again, and we have a new message: `ReferenceError on line: 5: "t" is not defined`.

We have created a known stable wrapper for any code we insert between the `try` and `catch` that will give detailed information about errors that occur at runtime. Next we will extend this container and set breakpoints to help us understand what is happening during a run.

Break and Report

Sometimes you need to test out what a service or other operation is returning in order to build the UI. Other times an error may be because of the values being fed to the failing code. When we talk about "breaking the code," we mean that you will stop the run at a certain point so you have an opportunity to see what values exist at that point.

Following the preceding example, let's test the value of x before setting it to the undefined t value. Replace the code between the `try/catch` with the following:

```
...
    var x=5;
    html.setContent("Value of x is: " + x);
```

```
    return html;

    var x=t;
  ...
```

Remember that JavaScript is a top-down language. Therefore, each line runs one after the other. Certainly you can run a function that may be at the very end of the code and then come back to the top, but the order of execution will always be line by line: there is no "go-to line 9" in JavaScript.

In the new code, the value of x is set to 5. Next we will output the message of what x is now. The error of t not being defined still exists, but that code will not be executed because the service is returned (breaks) before that line runs. Therefore, we will only see the message: `Value of x is: 5`. You might ask, why not just use `Logger.log` and read it in the Script Editor? That's a good idea as long as you're accessing the app as you, and running it yourself. If the app is being run by someone else, you will not see logs. Next we will talk about dealing with that issue from a production standpoint.

Production Error Logging

Debugging is essential during development, but keep in mind it will only catch what *you* expect, and your users will always find ways to use your product in ways you would not have thought possible. This section will discuss how to keep track of problems in your apps that are out in the wild, untamed user realm.

Logging the Backend

The concept is simple: use a `try/catch` statement like the one in "Handling Errors and Breaks" on page 26, but with the twist of logging each error in a spreadsheet. I would like to note that if you are the twitchy type, you can also have errors emailed directly to you as they occur. I don't recommend this, because it is hard to sift through emails and detect patterns when a spreadsheet lists the failures in the order they occurred. If you want an email to let you know things have gone awry, you can always set the spreadsheet notification feature to send an email.

Here's the setup:

1. Create a new spreadsheet and rename the first sheet "errors."

   This will be the place for logging errors. You must make sure that the account running the script has editor permissions to your spreadsheet.

2. Get the spreadsheet ID from the URL, which will look something like this:

   ```
   https://spreadsheets0.google.com/a/example.com/spreadsheet/ccc?key=0Aq1-
   MXh5T0c3NVE&amp;hl=en_US#gid=0
   ```

   The `0Aq1-MXh5T0c3NVE` part is your spreadsheet's ID.

3. Modify the code from "Handling Errors and Breaks" on page 26 by inserting the following code. Be sure to insert your unique spreadsheet ID:

```
}catch(error){
  var errorSheet = SpreadsheetApp.openById('<Your Spreadsheet ID>')
    .getSheetByName('errors');
  var cell = errorSheet.getRange('A1').offset(errorSheet.getLastRow(),0);
  cell.setValue(new Date() + " function doGet: " + error);
}
```

Because you are now accessing the Spreadsheet Service, you need to select the doGet function and click "Run" so you can grant permission. If you don't, in the web app page you will see "Authorization is required to perform that action." Any time you see this it should be a cue to run the app from the editor once.

Now when you run the script, errors will be written to the spreadsheet row by row (see Figure 2-2). Adding timestamps also helps identify why something may be failing.

Figure 2-2. Spreadsheet for recording errors

Logging HTML Frontends

When we run an application in the UiApp Service or as code in the editor, we are mainly doing server-side execution. We have lots of tools for debugging and error tracking when we run the script from the editor. However, when we start running the HTML Service, that code is run in the client's browser rather than on the Google server, where we can check the logs to see if something has gone wrong. Yes, you can run the code in your browser to test, and use some of the great tools like the JavaScript Console to figure out problems. The question becomes, what will you do to diagnose problems when they arise after you release your application to the world?

I would like to show you a method that should help you find out two things about your app: one, whether your deployed app is failing in some way, and two, where to look for the problem. Let's start by copying the script from "Hello Web App" on page 16. This will give us a basic working example.

Go ahead and run through publishing the script and getting the dev version loaded in a new window. Now open the JavaScript Console so you will be able to see the error we are going to induce. Open the *index.html* file in the Script Editor, and add this line between the `script` tags:

```
hiUser("Welcome guest!");
```

The entire file should now look like this:

```
<html>
  <head>
    <script>
        hiUser("Welcome guest!");
    </script>
  </head>
  <body>
    <div>Hello Web App</div>
  </body>
</html>
```

Go to the web app's page and reload the page. Now you will see an error like the one shown in Figure 2-3.

```
×   Elements  Resources  Network  Sources  Timeline  Profiles  Audits  Console
  ▶ SES initialization
    Sandbox mode: NATIVE
  ⊗ ▶TypeError: undefined is not a function
  ›
```

Figure 2-3. An error in the JavaScript Console

This is telling us that there is a problem with an `undefined` that thinks it's a function. That is true; we never created a function called `hiUser`. OK, we know what is wrong, and I'm sure all our users will be overjoyed to send detailed reports of what they've found in the JavaScript Console. Trust me, some will: however, we should know there is a problem and be dealing with it before users get involved.

 As of this writing the HTML Service is using Caja, which makes a mess of the output and seems to strip out a few tools. One of those is `error.line`, which is available in most browsers. Currently the only thing you will get is `error.message`.

What we are going to do is write this error to the spreadsheet we used in "Logging the Backend" on page 28. Open the *Code.gs* file and append this code:

```
function logErrors(e){
  var errorSheet = SpreadsheetApp.openById('<Your Spreadsheet ID>')
    .getSheetByName('errors');
  var cell = errorSheet.getRange('A1').offset(errorSheet.getLastRow(),0);
  cell.setValue(new Date() + " : " + e);
}
```

This is a function that does the same thing we did earlier in the chapter and takes one argument, the error. To implement this we need to go to the *index.html* file and add a special Google Apps Script call inside the `script` tags as well, and wrap the error in a `try/catch`. Here is what the whole code block will look like:

```
<html>
  <head>
    <script>
    try{
        hiUser("Welcome guest!");
    }catch(e){
        google.script.run.logErrors(e.toString());
    }
    </script>
  </head>
  <body>
    <div>Hello Web App</div>
  </body>
</html>
```

We use `google.script.run.<functionName>` to do things on the server side. We will get into this much more as we start building apps later in the book. For now, know that we are simply passing the error `e` to the function created in *Code.gs*.

 When you pass a value in the argument using `google.script.run.<functionName>` it must be a string, or you will get an error similar to this in the JavaScript Console: `TypeError: Failed due to illegal value in property: 0`. If you do need to pass something like an object, use `JSON.stringify(value)` and, in the *Code.gs* file, `JSON.parse(text)` to turn it back into an object.

Go to your web app page and reload it. There should be no errors in the JavaScript Console now, and if you open your "errors" spreadsheet, you will see that a new line has been written that looks like what's shown in Figure 2-4.

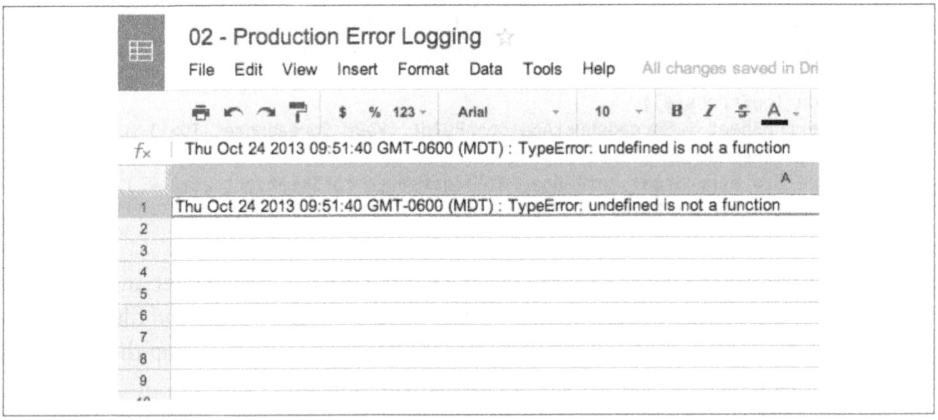

Figure 2-4. Frontend error log in a spreadsheet

Wrapping Up

In this chapter, you learned several ways to debug your code and keep track of problems in your script after deployment. Remember that users like to have useful information to give you when things have gone wrong. A generic error at the top of the page, or worse, seemingly nothing at all, will only frustrate the user and lessen the usefulness of your app. Often the best solution is to have the error reported to you so you can already have a plan in place before your users come looking for you.

You should always keep an eye out for places in your code where several things need to be processed and a failure would kill the whole run. Employ the `try/catch` in these cases, so that one failure is reported while the remaining tasks complete.

CHAPTER 3

Building an Interface

What's in a UI?

A user interface, or UI, is what you see when you turn on a computer. It may be an action-packed blockbuster movie or a single flashing green >, but one thing is for sure, this is the way you interact with the machine. When we talk about building a UI, we are typically speaking of the part that your user will need to interact with your application. Text to read, pictures to look at, boxes to type in, and buttons to push are what we call *elements*. We create our pages using standard HTML, and while we won't discuss HTML in depth here, O'Reilly has an excellent book covering the subject: Elisabeth Robson and Eric Freeman's *Head First HTML and CSS*.

When we build a UI in Google Apps Script, there are three ways to present the UI to the user: in a container such as a Google Doc or Sheet, in a Google Site as a gadget, or as a web page, which we call a web app. Please see Chapter 1 for a detailed description of each UI display type. For this chapter, the focus will be on the web app UI.

When you publish your web app UI, it gets a Google-hosted URL that looks something like *https://script.google.com/a/macros/<unique>* where you can access your HTML and JavaScript.

It Starts with doGet

In order to display a UI in your web app or Google Sites gadget, you must have a function called doGet that returns some HTML. When using a spreadsheet-integrated UI, you can call your function anything you like because of the way Google has done the wrapper.

We use the HTML Service (*http://bit.ly/html-service*) to create HTML to display on the page. The output from the HTML Service can be written in as a string and requires only a few lines of code:

```
function doGet() {
  var html = HtmlService.createHtmlOutput('<h2>Hello World</h2>');
  return html;
}
```

However, we have been in an HTML world for quite a long time, and creating HTML content as one long string would be extremely tedious. Lucky for us, Google has added the ability to create HTML pages as files in the Google Apps Script service. These pages are exactly like what you have always used, and with the exception of Caja limitations, most HTML can be dropped right in and run.

To call on one of these files, you must use the method createTemplateFromFile(<File Name>) or createHtmlOutputFromFile(<FileName>). I would say use the former most of the time, because it allows you to interact in much the same way you might use PHP to call on a backend server. If you know that everything is going to happen up front on the client side, then go ahead and use the latter. Here is what the whole thing looks like calling on a file named *index*:

```
function doGet() {
  var html = HtmlService.createTemplateFromFile('index').evaluate()
          .setTitle('Web App').setSandboxMode(HtmlService
                    .SandboxMode.NATIVE);
  return html;
}
```

There is a funny part on the end of the code above, setSandboxMode(HtmlService.Sand boxMode.NATIVE), which, according to Google, makes the HTML Service load faster. It is a good idea to always add it on, but at some point it may become the default.

Now that you know how to display a file, let's actually put one together and talk about some of the things you can do inside it. In the Script Editor, go to File→"New file"→ "Html file." Name it *index* and you will be ready to create some HTML, as shown in Figure 3-1.

Now add some HTML inside the div tags:

```
<div>
  <h2>Hello World</h2>
</div>
```

Save all your files, publish the app as shown in "Publishing options" on page 18, and load the dev page.

There you have it: the basics of presenting some objects to the user. Next up, we will build a real interface like those you have probably used on many web pages.

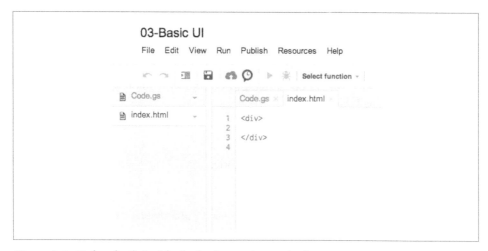

Figure 3-1. Only what's inside the body tags is required

Contact Me

Sales just called; they want you to add a Contact Me form on the website so the company can email news updates when something big happens. You could simply fire up the built-in form tool from Google Docs and insert one question with a text box, but there are a few things you don't like about that option. First, the Google form has extra information about it being a Google form, taking up extra space on the page. Second, you don't want the full-page "submitted" notification to pop up, because it takes the customer away from the site.

Thinking about your UI, you decide there will need to be a label to tell the users what to do, a text box for them to enter an email address, and a button to submit the form. You would like to verify that they've entered an email address and provide some kind of feedback if they did not. Finally, it would be nice to display that something has happened when they push the button by saying "Thank you."

In this chapter, we will create the UI, and in Chapter 4 we will implement the backend that performs the work once the submit button is clicked. Your company has gone Google, so you will need a Google Site to complete this example. Google Sites is open to all, so you have everything you need to get started.

Getting Started

You can build on the example we just completed or create a duplicate copy from the File menu. At the end of the chapter we will be inserting this app into a Google Sites page, so you can also build this script from the Manage menu in Google Sites, as shown in "Hello, Google Sites" on page 20.

The *Code.gs* file is already doing what it should, so leave it alone for now and let's focus on *index.html*. Basically, you need a form element, which is common HTML.

 Google claims faster load times if you don't use <head> and <body> tags, so we will not be using those, unlike what you might see on a normal HTML page.

In your *index.html* file, insert the following code:

```
<div id="subscribe_form">
  <form>
    <input type="email" name="email" id="email" placeholder="Enter your email">
    <input type="submit" value="Subscribe">
  </form>
</div>
```

We know that it's an email address that we want to get from the user, and normally that would require doing some sort of validation using JavaScript. However, that can get really complicated. Save yourself a headache and go with HTML5. Yes, you're in luck, most HTML5 is supported in the HTML Service. This means that form validation for something like an email address simply requires using the type="email" property.

Now do a quick test by loading up your latest code in a browser window and typing in part of an email address, as shown in Figure 3-2, then clicking the Subscribe button. Yeah HTML5!

Figure 3-2. Email validation

Next you will need an element to thank the user for making the effort to sign up for your great stuff. This can be accomplished in many ways, but in this case we can use a span element just inside the closing div, as shown in the following snippet:

```
...
<span id="thank_you">Thank you!</span>
</div>
```

If you reload the dev page, you now have the thank you message showing just under the input box. In the next chapter we will add the code that is going to show that thank you, and later in this chapter we will hide it, but first we need to add some style.

Adding style

Your UI looks OK… well, actually it is a bit ugly, so let's add some style to it by creating a CSS file. In the Editor menu, click "File"→ "New file"→"Html file" and name the file "CSS." I know you might be thinking that it's not really an HTML file, but don't worry: it will work fine for us.

To load this file on the page, we can call on the Google Apps Script HTML Service by using scriptlets that look like this: <?= *your_code* ?>. There are two different types of scriptlets: printing, which use the equals sign, and nonprinting, without. What's the difference? Importing our CSS file will be a perfect example. When you use a printing scriptlet, it writes on the HTML page and will act just like you typed out the same thing on the page itself.

Here is the code to pull in the code from the *CSS.html* file. Put it under the closing div in the *index.html* file:

```
<?!= HtmlService.createHtmlOutputFromFile('CSS').getContent(); ?>
```

When you want to add style to an HTML page, you surround the CSS in <style> tags. It is also this way with our *CSS.html* file, and after reading the last few paragraphs the pieces should be coming together. Here is the CSS to put in the *CSS.html* file:

```
<style>

div {
    width:300px;
    margin: 50px auto;
    background-color: #fff;
    border:1px solid #000;
    padding:10px;
    text-align:center;
}

#thank_you {
    font-family: Verdana, sans-serif;
    font-size:30px;
    color: #0000FF;
}

</style>
```

Reload the page and you will see a much improved look, as shown in Figure 3-3.

Figure 3-3. "Thank you" with style

The last part of code we need is to hide the thank you. We do this with a simple attribute added to the span element, `hidden="true"`.

Here is the final code for the *index.html* file:

```
<div>
  <form id="email_subscribe">
    <input type="email" name="email" id="email" placeholder="Enter your email">
    <input type="submit" value="Subscribe">
  </form>
  <span id="thank_you" hidden="true">Thank you!</span>
</div>

<?!= HtmlService.createHtmlOutputFromFile('CSS').getContent(); ?>
```

The last part of the UI is to add it to the Google Sites page. So far we have been using the dev version, but in order to display to your users you will need to publish a new version of your app. In the Script Editor, click "File"→"Manage versions." This opens the Manage Versions window so you can snapshot the latest changes (Figure 3-4).

Click the "Save New Version" button. You can put in a reason for the new version, but it's not required. After the window closes, click "Publish"→"Deploy as web app" and change the project version to the latest build. Click the "Update" button to make that version live. On the next screen, copy the contents of the "Current web app URL" field.

Manage Versions

A version is a snapshot of your project that can be used as a library in other projects.

Describe what has changed...   Save New Version

Version	Description	Saved By	Date
2		james@simpleappssolutions.com	2013-11-08 16:09
1		james@simpleappssolutions.com	2013-11-06 15:20

OK

Figure 3-4. The Manage Versions window

Inserting the gadget into your site is really very easy. Open the home page of your site and click the Edit icon (a pencil). In the menu bar that appears, choose "Insert"→"Apps Script." Paste your web app URL in the box at the bottom and click the Select button. Save a few times to get back out to the live page, and you're done.

The "Manage Versions" feature gives you the power to roll out an update and, if things go badly, very quickly go right back to a working version.

There you have it: a form with email validation ready to start taking in data—well, almost. Now that you do have a form, in the next chapter we will learn how to use jQuery and sever-side functions to actually record the data.

CHAPTER 4

Adding Actions

In Chapter 3, you began creating an application to collect email addresses from visitors who would like you to contact them. The only problem is that clicking your "Subscribe" button doesn't do anything yet. In this chapter, we will add actions to that button to store the visitors' email addresses, thank them if they entered an email address, and send them an email verification.

Handling User Actions

In order to work, a button needs an event handler. However, buttons are not the only elements that can have handlers, and click is not the only handler type. For example, a text box may have a handler that responds to the user pressing the Enter key, or a listbox sometimes needs to fill a second list for situations like choosing a city after the state has been selected. In such a case, we might use an onChange handler. In more advanced UIs, mouse handlers like over and off can create rich user interaction by displaying information before a selection is made. It's also important to note that an element can have more than one handler. When you have a process that may take some time, like receiving data from a web service or uploading files from the hard drive, it's a good idea to show a progress indicator to the user after he has clicked, and an additional handler may take care of that detail.

In this chapter, we will keep things simple and only work with the submit handler to provide action for our simple form.

Anatomy of a Handler

Google Apps Script allows us to use jQuery, which is the preferred technique in HTML programing to date. I highly recommend learning as much jQuery as possible. In the long run, it will save you countless hours of trying to figure out how to write something in pure JavaScript—because that thing has already been included in jQuery and can be accomplished by simply pasting in a single command.

Let's start where we left off in Chapter 3 by opening our existing Contact Me code. The first thing we need to do is import the jQuery library into our *index.html* file. You can import the jQuery library in a number of different ways, such as by saving a copy on your server or in Google Drive. There are quite a few publicly available custom versions, but because Google Apps Script uses Caja and can be very picky about any imported code, I recommend using a particular version provided by Google.

To import this version of jQuery, add the following line of code to the end of your *index.html* file:

```
<script src="//ajax.googleapis.com/ajax/libs/jquery/1.9.1/jquery.min.js">
</script>
```

Now that we have installed jQuery, let's add an event to the "submit" button. We want the page to always display as quickly as possible, and we want to avoid any issues with a browser that might try to load things in a strange order. When we want to add an event to any object on the page, that object must be there to attach to, or the process will fail. The safest way to accomplish this is to use the jQuery `ready` method, which will watch for the page to be fully loaded before it starts executing JavaScript.

The `ready` method looks like this:

```
$( document ).ready(function() {
    console.log( "ready!" );
});
```

To attach our event handler to the button, we will use the `submit` method because it will detect a mouse click or Enter keypress. Again, this is one of those examples where jQuery saves us a line of code to take care of a simple task.

Add the following code to the end of your *index.html* file:

```
<script>
  $( document ).ready(function() {
    $( "#email_subscribe" ).submit(function() {
      $( "#thank_you" ).show();
    });
  });
</script>
```

Now let's break that down. After the page is loaded and ready, we use the jQuery $ to get the Document Object Model (DOM), which you can think of as all the code on the page, to get the form element by its ID. If you look in the HTML section of the *index.html* code, we used `<form id="email_subscribe">` to identify the form itself. Now we can call on it by name:

```
$( "#email_subscribe" )
```

Calling Elements

jQuery uses CSS style tags to identify the elements, which has the dual purpose of making it easy to use and allowing you to style and use elements with less code. However, when you call on an element you must use the form id=<name> and . for class=<name>. This way jQuery knows what it's looking for and why you see the # to access ("#email_subscribe").

Next we attach the submit method to the form. This method takes a function to perform tasks, and we will be unhiding the "Thank you" message by again using jQuery to get the #thank_you span element and asking jQuery to *show* it.

Save your work and give it a test by loading the "latest code" dev link. You now have a working "submit" button, and we are performing actions on the page. In the next section we will start working with server-side callbacks in order to process the data to a spreadsheet.

Here is the full code for *index.html* so far:

```
<div>
  <form id="email_subscribe">
    <input type="email" name="email" id="email" placeholder="Enter your email">
    <input type="submit" value="Subscribe">
  </form>
  <span id="thank_you" hidden="true">Thank you!</span>
</div>

<?!= HtmlService.createHtmlOutputFromFile('CSS').getContent(); ?>
<script src="//ajax.googleapis.com/ajax/libs/jquery/1.9.1/jquery.min.js">
</script>

<script>
  $( document ).ready(function() {
    $( "#email_subscribe" ).submit(function() {
      $( "#thank_you" ).show();
    });
  });
</script>
```

The Concept of the Callback

When your app needs to do something—like update information on the screen, add data to a spreadsheet, or send an email—it performs what is known as a *remote procedure call*, or RPC for short. An RPC includes sending code to the server for processing, referred to as a *call*, and having the server send back the results, known as a *callback*. I am sure that Java developers are pulling their hair out at this simplistic definition of RPCs, but for what you need to know in Google Apps Script, this about covers it.

In our case, we will want to get the input from the text box and write it to a spreadsheet. This means we need to construct a call from our *index.html* file and pass our text box value to a function in the *Code.gs* file, which we can consider as our server. To make it a little easier to understand, let's get the server-side part started, so there is something to refer to when making the call.

Open up the *Code.gs* file and add this function:

```
function addEmail(form){
    Logger.log(form.email);
    return 200;
}
```

This is a simple function that will let us know that we are indeed getting a response from the server. Remember that you will only be able to check the log if you run the app, but for our case we are going to return the value 200, which is the web standard for a successful execution.

You can pass JavaScript and other elements in the server request. Google Apps Script is smart enough to know that the elements in a form can be converted to object properties. In this example we will pass the form element, which means we can access the child elements by calling form.<name>.

Now, back in the *index.html* file, it's time to make the call by modifying the submit function. Google Apps Script has a few special ways to run an RPC, but the one we will use most of the time looks like this:

```
google.script.run.withSuccessHandler(serverResponseFunction).serverFunction-
Name();
```

What we are doing is calling a server function in one of our *.gs* files; if it does not send back an error, we run a function here on the client side to process whatever the server returned.

If the server does find an error, then it will log it in the JavaScript Console. You can change this behavior by using .withFailureHan dler and then doing something to notify the user.

Replace $("#thank_you").show(); within the submit method function with the following code:

```
google.script.run.withSuccessHandler(function(ret){
        console.log(ret);
    }).addEmail(this);
```

Here we are asking to run a function called addEmail on the server, which we will pass the whole form: i.e., this. If you look back at the submit handler, you'll see that we attached it to the form so that when the button is clicked this represents the form. If the server call is successful, when we get the callback we will run the function within the withSuccessHandler arguments. Because we expect a return value, we add the argument ret to represent what's returned. It can be just about any JavaScript element.

Just to check out the functionality, we will give a little output to the JavaScript Console. Be sure you know how to open the JavaScript Console on your browser, because we use it a bunch when building frontends.

At this point you can save your work and reload the dev page. In the JavaScript Console you will see a 200, as shown in Figure 4-1.

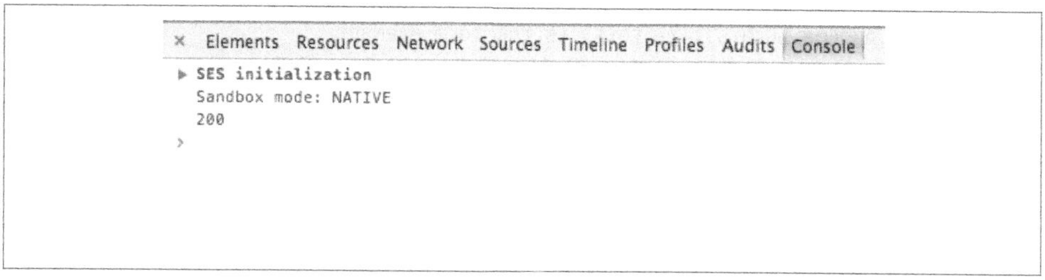

Figure 4-1. Logging in the JavaScript Console

Believe it or not, the frontend and user actions are almost done. All we need now is to hide the form and display the "Thank you" with a little style. Just above the console.log line, add:

```
$( "#thank_you" ).show("slow");
$("#email_subscribe").slideUp();
```

Now give it a whirl, and you have finished the user experience side of this application (see Figure 4-2).

Thank you!

Figure 4-2. The final user view

That was a lot to cover, so here is what the entire code for *index.html* looks like:

```
<div>
  <form id="email_subscribe">
    <input type="email" name="email" id="email" placeholder="Enter your email">
```

```
      <input type="submit" value="Subscribe">
    </form>
    <span id="thank_you" hidden="true">Thank you!</span>
  </div>

  <?!= HtmlService.createHtmlOutputFromFile('CSS').getContent(); ?>
  <script src="//ajax.googleapis.com/ajax/libs/jquery/1.9.1/jquery.min.js">
  </script>

  <script>
    $( document ).ready(function() {
      $( "#email_subscribe" ).submit(function() {

        google.script.run.withSuccessHandler(function(ret){
          $( "#thank_you" ).show("slow");
          $("#email_subscribe").slideUp();
          console.log(ret);
        }).addEmail(this); //"this" is the form element

      });
    });
  </script>
```

Functions Are Where the Action Happens

Applications built on the server side in Google Apps Script have four basic types of functions: doGet, which you are familiar with; doPost, which you will learn about later; functions that return values directly; and functions that are intended to be used via a trigger. They aren't really that different; however, *when* you use them can be important. For example, you always need doGet to display the UI in a gadget or web app, and if you are using a form from a different service, you will likely need a doPost function.

When you operate a function using an event handler and your intent is to send some information to the server, you must use google.script.run.

Storing the Values

I have saved the best for last—or maybe the easiest part, depending on how you look at it. The app you have been building has all the features needed to interact with the user, but we are lacking the most important thing: a place to store the data and a way to get it there. Not to worry: Google has provided us with several data-storage options that should work for most applications. One great option is a spreadsheet, and this is typically where you would store data like this. Next, there is ScriptDB, which we will get to later in the book. Another option for very important or very large sets of data is Cloud SQL. This is an excellent service and requires payment, but the cost is small given all the features.

Storing in a Spreadsheet

If you have been following along, your script is living on a Google Site, and you have been accessing it through the published URL. What we need to do now is write the visitor's email address to a spreadsheet. First, we will need a spreadsheet, so please open Google Sheets and make one. You can name it anything you like.

Setting Up the Spreadsheet

The top row of our spreadsheet will be the column names, so we know what the data is. (Yes, it is obvious for such a small app, but you know how things can grow.) In column A1 (top left), name the column "Time Stamp." Next, name B1 "Email." See Figure 4-3 for an example.

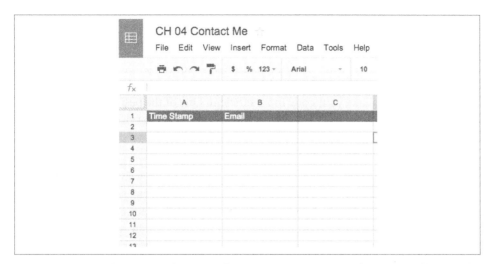

Figure 4-3. Spreadsheets can be set up for storing values much like one would use a database

Heading back to your script, you will need to add the code to open your new spreadsheet in the script so you can write the email values to it.

In the *Code.gs* file, above the line `Logger.log(form.email);`, insert:

```
var ss = SpreadsheetApp.openByUrl('<YourSpreadsheetUrlGoesHere>')
.getSheets()[0];
```

Here we are creating a variable, `ss`, that will represent the first sheet in our spreadsheet. SpreadsheetsApp is a Google Apps Script service, like the HTML Service. Having built-in services that we can call on in the same script makes using Google Apps Script so easy. Next we will use the `openByUrl` method to get the sheet where we need to write data. Simply skip over to your spreadsheet and copy the URL from the address bar.

What is a spreadsheet ID, you may be asking yourself? In Google Docs, everything—including pictures, PDFs, presentations, and spreadsheets—has a unique ID by which it can be tracked. Fortunately, these IDs are very easy to find. Select your spreadsheet and look in the address bar where the URL is. Find key=. The long string from there up to # is the unique ID. When you want to open a document or spreadsheet you can use .openById and this unique ID. Alternatively, you can use .openByUrl, as we have done here. It should look something like this, with the URL in quotes:

```
.openByUrl("https://docs.google.com/a/apps4gaaps.com/spreadsheet/ccc?key=0Aq1-
           C9Nl4dO-dHzM9fdXlLV1E#gid=0")
```

The last part of the code string, .getSheets()[0], simply gets the sheet furthest to the left, or the first one. Note that this is a zero-based call because .getSheets returns an array of the sheets in the spreadsheet. This is an application built to do just one thing, and it will have only one sheet, but if you are concerned that your sheet may move to a different place, it would be a good idea to use .getSheetByName(name). This way it doesn't matter where the sheet is, just as long as the name stays the same.

It can be useful to know when a visitor submitted a request, so we will need to create a timestamp to go along with the email. When using Google Apps Script, it's always good to look for ways to make your code more efficient. One of the best ways to do this is to minimize the number of calls you make to any of the other services, inside or outside of Google. While you can certainly write the data to a spreadsheet one cell at a time, you will likely run into timeout issues, and it'll take forever.

The next thing we need to do is get the range of cells where we want to write our values. When accessing a spreadsheet you get the cells with the getRange method. There are several constructors for the method, such as using "A1" notation, where the column letter and row number are used much the same way they are in spreadsheet formulas (as in A1 or A1:C6). Letters can get confusing, so there is also a constructor that accepts numbers in place of the column letters. We will use .getRange(<row>, <column>, <numRows>, <numColumns>):

```
var range = ss.getRange(ss.getLastRow()+1, 1, 1, 2);
```

ss.getLastRow returns the number of the last row of data. We want to write our new submission to the row after that, so we simply add one (+1). Next, we want to start a column, so <column> is represented by a 1. There is only one row of data to write, but with the date, it is going to be two columns wide, hence the 1 and 2 at the end of the set.

 When converting columns from letters to numbers, the first column is number one, A=1. However, after you get the values, they will be in a JavaScript array that is zero-based, meaning column A is now zero, not one.

Setting Up the Data

The data will need to be placed in what is known as a *2D array*, so that we only need to write to the spreadsheet once. Here is how that looks: `[[row1 column1, row1 column2] , [row2 column1, row2 column2]]`, and so on, as shown in Figure 4-4. Any amount of consecutive rows and columns can be written simultaneously in this way.

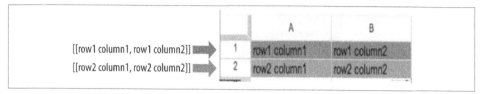

Figure 4-4. The getRange method creates a 2D array

Because we only have one row, the data looks like this:

```
var values = [[new Date(), form.email]];
```

Now that we have the range of cells and the data in a matching configuration, all that is left is to write it:

```
range.setValues(values);
```

Save your work and then click the "Run" button in the "Script Editor." You need to grant access to the SpreadsheetApp Service or face the wrath of an Auth error in the UI. Now load up the web app dev page. Remember that you need to use an email address in the form or the validation will trigger. After pressing the "submit" button, you should receive a "Thank you" message. In the spreadsheet, you will see the results of all your hard work over the last two chapters (Figure 4-5). Please refer to Chapter 1 for a refresher on placing the web app as a gadget in your site.

Here's the final code for the *Code.gs* file:

```
function doGet() {
  var html = HtmlService.createTemplateFromFile('index').evaluate()
             .setTitle('Ch4 Contact Me')
             .setSandboxMode(HtmlService.SandboxMode.NATIVE);
  return html;
}

function addEmail(form){
  var ss = SpreadsheetApp.openByUrl('<YourSpreadsheetUrlGoesHere>')
    .getSheets()[0];
  var range = ss.getRange(ss.getLastRow()+1, 1, 1, 2);
  var values = [[new Date(), form.email]];
  range.setValues(values);
  Logger.log(form.email);
```

```
    return 200;
}
```

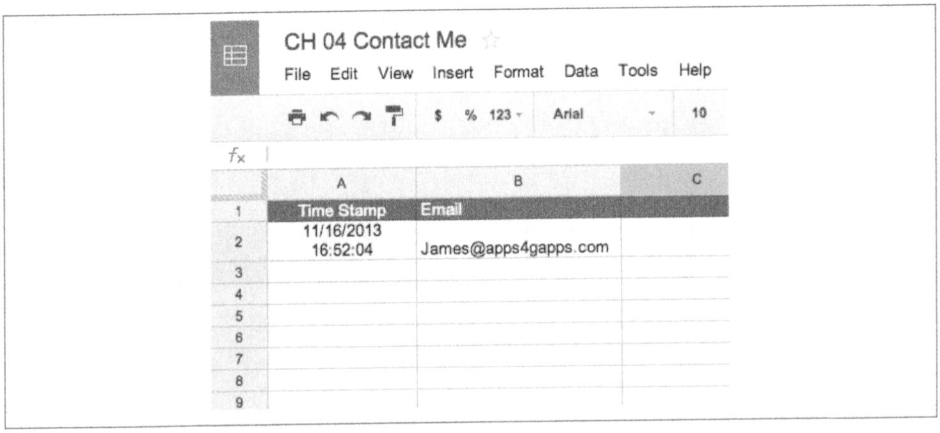

Figure 4-5. Each entry is saved in the spreadsheet and timestamped.

We have covered all the basics of displaying web apps and interacting with the Google Apps Script server, not to mention jQuery, CSS, and Google Sites. Take a deep breath and pat yourself on the back, then go grab some coffee. I recommend a `Star bucks.Grande().Black()`. In the next section of the book we will start creating some pretty complex applications: good luck to you, new Google Apps Script Developer!

Building Enterprise Applications

Dynamic Details: A Sites App Using HTML, CSS, and jQuery

Monday morning, finishing your last drops of coffee, you begin contemplating how there always seems to be a direct relationship between the power button on a computer and resolved help desk service tickets. Suddenly, Frank, the middle manager with a propensity for last-minute drama about any project requiring more than a paper clip, bursts into your cubicle, breathless and ranting. Between his wheezes, you discern that there is a problem with the new product information pages. "Too wordy, too cluttered, and too darn difficult to understand" are the sharper points of his reproach. Most of all, "the others"—his euphemism meaning the rest of the sales world—have fantastic look-ing pages. "How could we have let this slide, and why didn't we see it coming?" he laments. With a few gentle words, you calm Frank to a point of incoherent babbling and send him back to his office with a promise that you will do something to fight off those meanies and save the company from utter destruction.

Fighting Clutter

As more and more information is added to a web page, it becomes a jumble of images and text that flow together, losing the reader in a jungle of clutter, slashing away with the mouse pointer in an attempt to find that one key fact. We all want to keep the customers coming back for more, and that requires us to ensure they have a great ex-perience when visiting our sites. While we want to provide abundant information to persuade the customers that they are dealing with a knowledgeable supplier, too much information can cause them to miss what they are seeking.

Customers are visual browsers when it comes to choosing products. After all, a catalog is worthless without pictures of products, and your website is an online catalog. Often, the better visual presentation you make for a product, the more sales it will generate. A good way to gauge what you present to customers is by comparing it with big media providers like Netflix and YouTube. These megaretailers have discovered that they can pack more items on a web page by moving the description and purchasing mechanism to a pop-up panel, thus gaining more product impressions per page view. Figure 5-1 shows an example of displaying six items where a traditional web page would only have room for two.

Figure 5-1. An optimized web page, showing more content to the viewer than a traditional layout

When shopping on the Web, we naturally look for the picture of an item first; it's likely hard-wired into our hunter-gatherer genes to do so. For example, have you ever begun a web search for "beautiful sunset pictures" by reading descriptions about sunsets? No, you go to the images straight away. I know you also read reviews about products, but if something strikes your fancy, your next thought is most likely, "What does it look like?" Displaying more items on a page becomes very important to the user's experience, and that is what this chapter is all about. As you work through this chapter, keep in mind that there are three major components: the image repository, the database, and the products gadget, which is embedded into the Google Site.

What You Will Learn

You will learn how to:

- Use script gadgets in Google Sites
- Work with CSS
- Dynamically add elements to the page
- Work with the Google Sites Service
- Build powerful visual effects
- Create JavaScript data objects
- Use public classes

Supplies

You will need:

- A Google Site
- Product images
- Product descriptions

Application Overview

Your task is to help Frank keep his sanity by building an application that can be embedded into the company's Google Site and maximizing page space, showing as many products as possible to the customers while supplying them the information they need to make a wise purchase. A complete working example (*http://goo.gl/eGjEUc*) of this project is available online.

Image File Repository

There are as many ways to keep a product list as there are websites listing products, so if you already have your system in place, you will need to do some research on how web service–friendly it is. Google Apps Script gives you the ability to connect to databases and to SOAP and WSDL services, like the Amazon Web Services client, JSON, and all of the Google API services. To keep things simple and get you developing right away, we will use all Google services to set up your products page.

Load up your Google Site or create a new one, and create a new file cabinet page called "Products." Figure 5-2 shows an example of the Products image repository. This is where you will store the image files for each product, so get busy with the "Add file" button.

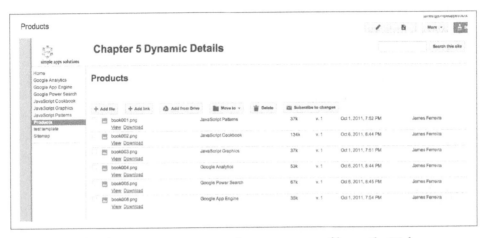

Figure 5-2. File cabinet pages are a convenient way to store files on the Web

Keep in mind that we will be setting the dimensions of the images in the UI, but it is a good idea to size all of your product images at nearly the same dimensions, and at the largest settings you will use to display them. This way you can avoid ugly pixelated images that will cause your boss to fume and customers to avert their eyes in disgust. You don't need to add descriptions here in the image repository, but they can be helpful when identifying what you are working with months from now.

Setting Up the Database

Whether you are a web designer by trade or the designated IT geek in the office, you are likely too busy to keep up with and maintain every aspect of the company's website. In the past, it took a webmaster and her secret ways to make every change required to keep the website current. In the fast-changing Web of today, that is simply more work than any one person should be tasked with. What if you get sick or go on vacation? Will you teach someone to hardcode each product into the website? Heck no, and this is why you need a database that is easy for staff to understand, simple to update, and able to automatically roll out changes to the website. Surprisingly, a spreadsheet is an excellent choice for this task because there is little to no training required to use it.

There are four main product elements you need to share with your customers: the image, the title, the description, and the link to more information. Certainly additional elements, such as customer ratings, similar products, and category information, are also excellent options to consider, and I encourage you to add them; you will have the skills for that soon.

Open a new spreadsheet and name it "Product Database." Name the columns "ID," "Title," "Description," "Image URL," and "Product Page," as shown in Figure 5-3.

Figure 5-3. Spreadsheet set up as a database for the image repository

You now have an image repository and a database. Next you will make entries in the database that represent each product.

Loading the Database

A very good reason for using a spreadsheet for your database is because they are familiar to most office workers, which means you can delegate maintaining the products page to anyone, even people outside of IT-like sales. A spreadsheet is easy to use, and in the case of a Google spreadsheet, you will be able to update the website from anywhere, including your cell phone. This brings me to another point: there is a two-step process going on here, where pictures are loaded to a site and then the spreadsheet is updated. I have set it up this way to keep the content of this chapter at a reasonable level, but later on in the book you will learn techniques for building a UI that uploads files and allows for describing them, essentially reducing the two steps in this chapter to one.

The ID column contains the product's unique identifier, meaning the same number should never appear more than once in that column. Skip over this for now, as we have something special ahead.

Next, the Title column contains the name of the product. It should be short, one word if possible, so that it fits well in our scheme. The title will appear in two places in the UI: once under the image and again in the pop-up information panel. The size of the text will be much different for each instance of the title, and that will be accomplished using CSS.

For the description, you will want a paragraph that is concise and provides just enough information for the customer to decide if this is the product he is looking for. One of the problems with the traditional web page is that each time you click a product, you are taken to a different page. Depending on connection speed, this can get monotonous and frustrate customers who have to constantly move up to the back arrow immediately after making a selection. The effect you are seeking will use mouseovers to show and hide each product's details. This approach allows the customer to quickly zero in on the specific item he is looking for and allows you to reap the benefits of his happy return to find more merchandise.

The simplest way to get the image URL is by right-clicking on the view link in the repository and selecting "Copy link address." At the end of the URL you may see ? attredirects=0. This can be removed or left alone, as it will not affect the outcome.

The last column of this example is the Product Page column: it contains a URL that will take the user to more information, an opportunity to make a purchase, or both. There are several ways the product link can be used. For example, the mouseover image on the product listing page could use this link if the customer is certain she wants that item and would like to go directly to its page; a button on the pop-up panel gives her a second opportunity to click through. You will create these pages in the next section.

The order of the products is not important but the ID column values are; they must be unique, so the correct item can be selected later.

This handy function will help you create random numbers in the A column of your "Product Database" spreadsheet after you have filled out the other columns; just add it and give it a quick run to add the IDs:

```
function randomString() {
  var ss = SpreadsheetApp.getActiveSheet();
  var randomArray = new Array();
  var chars = "ABCDEFGHIJKLMNOPQRSTUVWXTZabcdefghiklmnopqrstuvwxyz";
  var string_length = 10;
  var lastRow = ss.getLastRow()-1;
  for (var j=0; j<lastRow; j++){
    var randomstring = '';
    for (var i=0; i<string_length; i++) {
      var rnum = Math.floor(Math.random() * chars.length);
      randomstring += chars.substring(rnum,rnum+1);
    }
    randomArray.push([randomstring]);
  }
  ss.getRange(2, 1, lastRow, 1).setValues(randomArray);
}
```

This function will not check to see if the IDs generated are unique, but the odds of coming up with the same ID in a 10-character string taken from 52 choices is…well, let's just say if you do get a duplicate, go buy a lottery ticket now.

If you are completely paranoid about ensuring you have truly unique values, insert a temporary column to the left of A and insert this formula in cell A1: =unique(B2:B<our last row number>). If you have the same total row values in column A as in column B, they are all unique. Delete the temporary column A.

The spreadsheet is now ready to go with all the data and unique IDs (Figure 5-4).

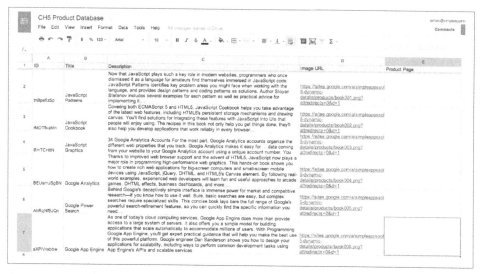

Figure 5-4. Product information has been entered

Creating Pages from a Spreadsheet

You have your unique IDs generated and your titles, descriptions, and image URLs entered in the "Product Database" spreadsheet. Now it is time to create all those individual web pages where the customer will go when he wants all the juicy details. You could begin the laborious process of creating each page one at a time from the Sites management service, but what if you have 100 or more products? This task would take days of tedious, repetitive work to complete. Wait a minute—Google Apps Script is built to automate Google products! Next, you will learn how to use Google Apps Script to create web pages and fill them with HTML content from a spreadsheet.

Using the Public Google Apps Script Objects Class

There are some tasks in Google Apps Script, like creating an object from a range of data in a spreadsheet, that use the same code regardless of the application you are writing. This is where open source libraries can be very handy. If you have done any JavaScript programming, you are likely familiar with jQuery, one of the most popular open source libraries for that language.

Google Apps Script is a young language, and there are not many references out there. In writing this book, the author felt it would be helpful to shorten your production time by creating several *libraries* to take care of the minutiae of coding common tasks. Having common, generic, open source code in one place is what makes languages great. You can find information about these open source classes on the Script Examples (*http://bit.ly/useful-libs*) website and the source code (*http://goo.gl/n8mQZa*).

In JavaScript, a library is typically saved as a *.js* file on your server and loaded using:

```
<script src="jquery.js"></script>
```

Because Google Apps Script is cloud-based, you will be storing the library code on Google's servers instead of your own. What's more, you can create and install libraries using the Scripts special key. Google has done a great job of explaining how to create your own library, so we won't go into that here. If contributing to the open source community is your thing, and I hope it is, then please read more about this subject under "Managing Libraries" in the Google Apps Script Development Environment Guide (*http://bit.ly/gas-libs*).

Using JavaScript Objects

One of the tasks we need to accomplish is turning the spreadsheet's rows of data into JavaScript objects to make them easier to use. Here is a comparison:

```
var spreadsheetData = [[firstName, LastName],[James, Ferreira],
                       [Homer, Simpson]]

spreadsheetData[1][1] //= Ferreira

//as an object

spreadsheetData[0].LastName //= Ferreira
```

You can see that converting our spreadsheet data to JavaScript objects they become a better option for performing operations later in the code.

Installing an Open Source Library

Start by creating a new script in the "Product Database" spreadsheet.

The library we need to install will make it easy to create our JavaScript objects; it can be found at ObjService (*http://bit.ly/objservice*) on the Google Script Examples site.

In the Script Editor, click "Resources" and select "Manage libraries" (Figure 5-5).

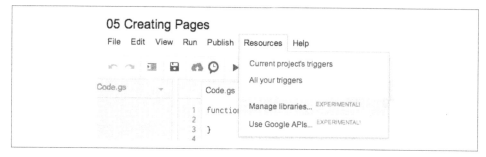

Figure 5-5. Installing an open source library

Paste the product key (`MTeYmpfWgqPbiBkVHnpgnM9kh30YExdAc`) into the "Find a Library" box and click the Select button. Now choose the latest version from the Version listbox. Clicking the Save button installs the library (Figure 5-6). Now that you have installed the library, note that it has the identifier *ObjApp*, which is how we will call the service from the code.

Figure 5-6. Library options

The title of the library is a link that will allow you to view the different methods included in that library and how it works.

To test the installation of the library, type `ObjApp.` in the Script Editor. When you hit the period key, the built-in autocomplete will show you what the library can do (see Figure 5-7).

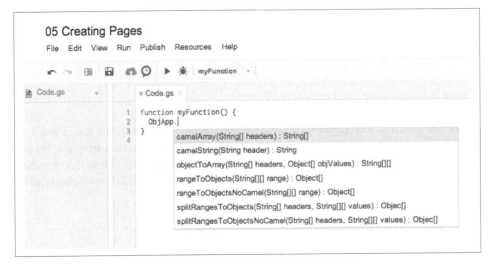

Figure 5-7. Autocomplete works in public libraries

Creating Pages and Filling the Spreadsheet

Creating a Google Sites page from Google Apps Script is easy because of the built-in Sites Service (*http://bit.ly/sites-serv*), which gives you access to create and change every aspect of a site. Automatically updating content, changing permissions, and pushing up new pages from custom templates that you design in the Sites manager are possible using the Sites Service.

To get our product pages automatically built, we will use a generic web page template, but if you are working from a site that is already built, feel free to look at the documentation and add the pages using a custom template.

The first thing we need to do is get the Google Site we want to work with. The following code gets the site as an object we can work with:

```
function createPages(){
  var site = SitesApp.getSiteByUrl('<Your Site URL>');
}
```

The `createWebPage(title, name, html)` (*http://bit.ly/class-page*) method is what you use to create pages in a site. The `title` argument is what you will see at the top of the page and in the navigation links. Don't confuse `title` with `name`, which is the page URL name. In the "Product Database" spreadsheet there is a column named "Title," which is what we want to display on our pages; in this simple use case, the URL might as well match the title. This may be fine in a real-world scenario depending on the titles you use, but spaces and special characters are not going to work well in a page URL, and the Script Editor will complain about invalid page names if you try to run it like that. Here is where ObjApp's `camelString(String)` method can help us out.

Throughout this book you will be pulling column headers, widget names, and IDs into your scripts. For this to work, they will need to be JavaScript-safe—more commonly referred to as *camelCase*. This means removing spaces, special characters, numbers at the beginning, and anything else that JavaScript might find obnoxious. To convert a string to camelCase, use:

```
ObjApp.camelString('Title');
```

Now that you know how to make the title, name, and description arguments safe, it's time to create pages by iterating through the rows of data in the spreadsheet. Well, sort of. There is one more problem: when you call `getRange` on a spreadsheet it will bring the data back just as it appeared in the spreadsheet, but in an array: `[[ID, Title, Description, Image URL, Product Page], [aLHeBRCUtT, JavaScript Patterns, Now...]]`. This way you can call out values as you would in any array.

 Spreadsheets start with 1, but arrays in your script are zero-based, meaning they start with 0. For example, consider `rangeArray[row][column]`. To get the value for row 2, column 2, you would write `rangeArray[1][1]`.

To get the title from column B, count A=0, B=1. This is fine in a very short script when you will be the only user, but let's say a friendly coworker comes along and rearranges your columns. The problem here with making an enterprise application is that it will be used every day and by many different people. You need to plan for some user-created issues. Furthermore, sooner or later you will run into an application that has columns CD, CE, etc., and out comes the calculator: 26*2+4... the headache continues. To solve this problem and keep your script from breaking, you need a way to get the values by asking for them by name and not the ambiguous column they are in.

JavaScript objects are something that it takes time to get your head around, but don't worry: the ObjApp library will do the work, allowing you to use the data without the fuss of figuring out how to create it. Here is how it works: get the data range that you want from the spreadsheet and use `rangeToObjects(range)` on the data array. Add the following lines to the bottom of your code, inside the closing }:

```
var ss = SpreadsheetApp.getActiveSheet();
var productDetails = ObjApp.rangeToObjects(ss.getDataRange().getValues());
```

Now what you have is an array of JavaScript objects that looks like this: `[aLHeBRCUtT, title=JavaScript Patterns, ...,{...}]`. Each element in the array is an object with property names made from the column headers (in camelCase, of course) that contains the values from each column. If you would like to get the title of the item in the third spreadsheet row, use:

```
productDetails[1].title    //don't forget arrays are zero-based
                           //and the header row has been removed
```

Keep in mind that the array is zero-based and that you are starting with the data rows, excluding the headers that are in row 1 (see Figure 5-8). Spreadsheet Row 1=headers, Row 2=first data row. Therefore, `productDetails[0]` is the first row of data.

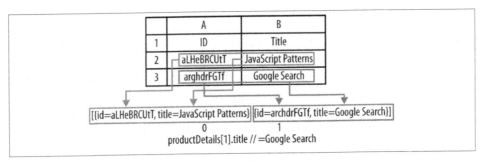

Figure 5-8. toDataObjects returns an array of row objects

Not only is this much easier to understand, it also solves the problems of moving columns around and counting up the alphabet. Don't forget that the object property representing the column header is in camelCase. If you are having problems figuring out what your column name has turned into, just run it through `Logger.log(camelString("Test Value"))`.

 The ObjApp library has methods for creating JavaScript objects that are not in camelCase if you have certain needs that fall outside this use case. Remember you will need to access these values as `javaObj[<Your Header>]`, not in the dot notation `javaObj.<yourHeader>`.

To create the pages, you will iterate through the `productDetails` object and build each page row by row. We have covered the `title` and page URL (`name`) arguments, but there is also the opportunity to create page content in the `html` argument. Because these are products and you have already stored the images, why not get a big head start on the detailed pages by automatically inserting the images and description text? If you use an additional "page template" argument, elements like purchasing, advertising, and other aspects could be applied too, giving you a finished presentation in this step. Save that for your homework; for now we will focus on the basics of creating a default web page and adding the content we have in the "Product Database" spreadsheet.

When writing the HTML page content, only focus on what would normally be inside the <body></body> tags. It is possible to add a variety of content this way, but with some limitations on scripting processes, which Google will kindly strip out. A script using an HTML template containing replaceable keys could achieve very complex effects. For the product pages you will use a very basic template that is built into the script and adds the image tags and descriptions.

Following is the for loop that creates the pages. It will be inserted after the last line of code in your script:

```
for (var i=0; i<productDetails.length; i++){
  var page = site.createWebPage(productDetails[i].title,
                                ObjApp.camelString(productDetails[i].title),
                                '<img src="'+productDetails[i].imageUrl+
                                '" align="left"/><p>'+
                                productDetails[i].description);
  productDetails[i].productPage = page.getUrl();
}
```

The productDetails object contains an entry representing each row in the data range. You iterate it by getting its length with productDetails.length and running the loop until the iterator i is larger than the length.

Next, create a variable page that will represent the web page returned by calling site.createWebPage. You could simply call on the Sites Service directly without a variable, but the database needs to know the page URL for each product, and you get that from the returned page object after the page is created. The arguments are filled in as discussed using the productDetails[i].<column header>.

The last line in the for loop works opposite to the others and inserts the page URL value into the productDetails[i].productPage property. This means that the productDetails object now contains new information that will need to be written back to the spreadsheet after the loop completes.

Why not write to the spreadsheet in the loop? Keep in mind that an RPC callback has to execute every time you write to the spreadsheet. Depending on how much data you have and the number of writes, this could take a very long time, and from the user's point of view it may appear that the application has become unresponsive. Always limit or group calls together for better performance.

The last step in the script will write the changed values back to the "Product Database" spreadsheet. Start by getting the headers: you never know, they might have changed in the last few milliseconds. In the next line, use the method objToArray from the ObjApp library to turn your productDetails object back into a spreadsheet range array:

```
var headers = ss.getRange(1,1,1,ss.getLastColumn()).getValues()[0];
var values = ObjApp.objectToArray(headers, productDetails);
ss.getRange(2, 1, values.length, values[0].length).setValues(values);
```

All that's left to do is write the values back to the spreadsheet. Because you used the spreadsheet headers to recreate the values, everything will line up in the correct column —how cool is that?

Save and run the script. You will see that the page URLs have filled in, and clicking one will open the product page, complete with an image and description, as shown in Figure 5-9.

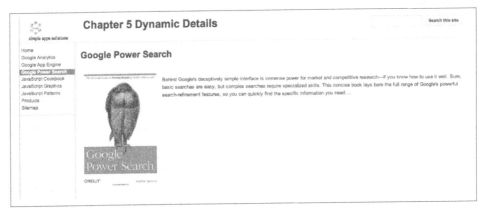

Figure 5-9. Automating page creation can save hours of time

Half a chapter later and you don't have a UI yet. Hang in there: before you can build a castle you need a solid foundation, and that is what you have built. The image repository, database, and product pages are ready to feed into the UI, which is where we are going next.

Here is the full code for the last section:

```
function createPages(){
  var site = SitesApp
    .getSiteByUrl(
        'https://sites.google.com/a/simpleappssolutions.com/chapter-5-dynamic-
details'
    );
  var ss = SpreadsheetApp.getActiveSheet();
  var productDetails = ObjApp.rangeToObjects(ss.getDataRange().getValues());
  for (var i=0; i<productDetails.length; i++){
    if (productDetails[i].productPage != "") continue;
    var page = site.createWebPage(productDetails[i].title,
                        ObjApp.camelString(productDetails[i].title),
                        '<img src="'+productDetails[i].imageUrl+
                        '" align="left"/><p>'+
```

```
                              productDetails[i].description);
    productDetails[i].productPage = page.getUrl();
  }
  var headers = ss.getRange(1,1,1,ss.getLastColumn()).getValues()[0];
  var values = ObjApp.objectToArray(headers, productDetails);
  ss.getRange(2, 1, values.length, values[0].length).setValues(values);
}

function randomString() {
  var ss = SpreadsheetApp.getActiveSheet();
  var randomArray = new Array();
  var chars = "ABCDEFGHIJKLMNOPQRSTUVWXTZabcdefghiklmnopqrstuvwxyz";
  var string_length = 10;
  var lastRow = ss.getLastRow()-1;
  for (var j=0; j<lastRow; j++){
    var randomstring = '';
    for (var i=0; i<string_length; i++) {
      var rnum = Math.floor(Math.random() * chars.length);
      randomstring += chars.substring(rnum,rnum+1);
    }
    randomArray.push([randomstring]);
  }
  ss.getRange(2, 1, lastRow, 1).setValues(randomArray);
}
```

Creating the Products UI

One feature of the Products UI is that items can be added to or removed from the database without needing to recode any of the components. Simply reloading the web page will cause the UI to reflect the changes. This makes it possible for you, the developer, to step away and allow less technical people to perform the data entry.

 The script you built earlier to create pages can handle figuring out which pages are already done, to avoid making duplicates. Add an `if` statement just inside the `for` loop to check the "empty" value in the Product Page column:

```
if (productDetails[i].productPage != "")
  continue;
```

The `continue` will simply skip to the next round in the loop if any value is found.

You can create a system that lets anyone manage your site's content from a spreadsheet. That way, those comfortable with spreadsheets but with little or no training on Google Sites will be able to control the information flow to the public.

Displaying Products

When beginning to develop a complex UI, it is helpful to break it down into smaller parts and build them one at a time. This modular approach is also helpful when you need to upgrade parts of the code. Breaking down this UI, there are product images to display with a certain number across the page and in rows continuing down. The title will go under each image and link to the product page. The next part happens when the mouse passes over the image. This will require a couple of handlers: one to display more information and another to hide the information when the mouse moves away from the image. You need something to display; therefore, building an information panel will be the next part. Finally, it will require CSS to get the whole page looking good and your information panel hovering over the other content.

For this section, the script will be written in the Sites Script Editor, allowing you to easily insert the UI as a gadget in any page.

Open your Products Site and create a new script.

As you work through the development steps, you can preview the UI using the web app dev page. You might also think about making a copy of our example from "Hello Web App" on page 16, which will have you ready to go in just a few minutes. Go ahead and publish the app so you can confirm that everything is working. If there are no errors, you can get started.

The next step will be to add the Object Service, as shown in "Installing an Open Source Library" on page 60. Here is the doGet function in the *Code.gs* file:

```
function doGet() {
  var html = HtmlService.createTemplateFromFile('index').evaluate()
      .setTitle('05 Dynamic Details')
      .setSandboxMode(HtmlService.SandboxMode.NATIVE);
  return html;
}
```

Products will be listed in rows down the page, and we may not know how many products are going to be in the database at any given time. Therefore, we will need to add the products dynamically.

The first thing we need to do is get the products from the spreadsheet so we can display them in a table on the page. To accomplish this, we will use the special Google Apps Script *Scriptlet* language.

Switch over to the *index.html* page and add these first lines of code:

```
<title>Chapter 5 Dynamic Details</title>
<? var data = getImages(); ?>
```

The first line is just the title of the page, but that second line is an interesting bit of code. As you learned in Chapter 1, the <? ?> tags enclose code we want to run directly on the

---

page. In this case we want to load all the data from the spreadsheet as objects that we can use later. Anything inside the scriptlets will run as if it was part of the code in the *Code.gs* file. You probably noticed a function; in there (`getImages`), which we will need to create.

> We could access the Spreadsheets Service from within the scriptlets, but later we will use the same function to return specific records. That requires sending information to the server, which can't be done in a scriptlet.

Now switch back to the *Code.gs* file, and we will build the function that handles retrieving data from the spreadsheet. Here is the whole function: we will go though each part so you can understand how it goes together:

```
function getImages(id){
  var ss = SpreadsheetApp.openByUrl('<Your Spreadsheet URL>').getSheets()[0];
  var data = ObjApp.rangeToObjects(ss.getDataRange().getValues());
  if(id){
    for (var i in data){
      if(data[i].id == id){
        return data[i];
      }
    }
  }else{
    return data;
  }
}
```

We know we need to do two things with this function. The first is to return all the data so we can list all the products on the home page. The second is to return just one specific record by its ID. For now, just create an `id` argument for the `getImages` function.

Recall that when we created the product pages on the Google Site we got the data from the spreadsheet and then turned it into JavaScript objects—that's how we get started here (see "Creating Pages and Filling the Spreadsheet" on page 62).

> Someone might want to move your sheets around, which will break your script. If you feel this might happen, name the sheet and use `.getSheetByName(`*name*`)` in place of `.getSheets()[0]`. You will still need to tell people not to change the name, so it's a tossup as to which approach will be most effective.

When our `getImages` function runs, it can take the argument `id`. If we want just one image, we pass the image ID in the argument, as in `getImages(`*imageidnumber123*`)`. If we want all the images we can leave out the argument (`getImages()`), and this will cause the value of id within the function to be undefined. if(id) will be true when an ID is supplied. Back in the *index.html* file, we used getImages(), which had no argument. Now we know that this is going to be false in our if statement, so we close this if statement with else and return all the data.

We will get to calling a specific record from the *index.html* page soon, but for now let's get the backend code done, so we don't need to come back here.

If there was a value passed in the argument, the if statement will be true. We are in control of what does get passed, and it will be one of those unique IDs. We use a for loop to iterate though the data, and when we match the record number we return just that record.

That's it for the *Code.gs* file. Now we can get started showing our products in the UI.

Creating the Products Table

The products are loaded into an object using the getImages method. Back in the *index.html* file we now have the data loaded into the data variable, and we can iterate through that to build a table to hold all the information.

Insert the following code at the end of the *index.html* file, and then we will go through it:

```
<? var j = 0;?>
<table cellpadding="20">
  <tr>
  <? for (var i = 0; i < data.length; i++) { ?>
     <?if(j==3){ ?>
        </tr><tr>
     <?   j=0
       }else{
          j++
       } ?>

     <td>
      <div><img id="<?=data[i].id?>" class="selector"
      src="<?=data[i].imageUrl?>"
      height="250" width="175"></div>
         <div class="book-titles"> <?= data[i].title ?></div>
      </td>
  <?} ?>
  </tr>
</table>
```

I know that having the scriptlets in there makes the code harder to read, but try to see past that. We want to have three products across the page and however many rows down until there is no more data. Going three wide is a bit of a trick that requires a variable to let us know when we get to three. There are a bunch of ways to do this in HTML, but

I chose using a table to show off some of the complexity that can be accomplished using scriptlets.

Create a table and the first row, then we'll start iterating. The first thing our code will run into is a check to see if our width variable has gotten to three. If it has, we start a new row and reset the width counter j to zero. If it hasn't, we will increment it.

Now we can add our first td, a.k.a. column. Inside the cell we will have an image and a title (see Figure 5-10).

Figure 5-10. Product layout

We will display more information using a pop-up dialog when the user mouses over the product image, but to know what information to dynamically load, we will need to know which product the user is over. Because the data object contains the unique product ID, what better reference could there be to use? In the image tag, set the id attribute using data[i].id. Similarly, use data[i].imageUrl to set the source. Getting the idea why we convert to JavaScript objects?

We will control the size here, so everything is the same size on the page, and lastly set the title. We keep adding to the table until there is no more data in the data object and then close off the table.

There is one more item we haven't added: the pop-up dialog. It's just a div with the id attribute dialog. Later we will be using jQuery UI to make it come alive:

```
<div id="dialog"></div>
```

Save your work and load the dev URL in your browser; your products will magically jump into place. At this point you have a typical database-driven products page like those common on the Web (Figure 5-11).

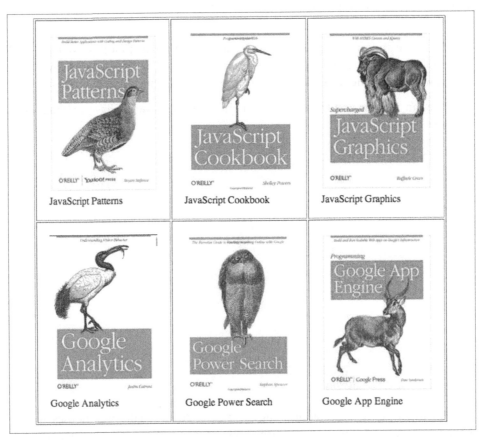

Figure 5-11. Products table

Adding Action

There are several event types: click events, for buttons and links; keypress events, which are useful in detecting the Enter key in a text box; and mouse events that will run when the mouse moves over or off your element. There are several more events, but for this application, the jQuery `mouseover` and `mouseleave` are used. I guess this would be a good time to load up Google's special versions of jQuery and jQuery UI:

```
<script src="//ajax.googleapis.com/ajax/libs/jquery/1.9.1/jquery.min.js">
</script>
<script src="//ajax.googleapis.com/ajax/libs/jqueryui/1.10.3/jquery-ui.min.js">
</script>
```

The rest of the code for the *index.html* page will be inside `script` tags, so add a few of those in which we can build the rest of the code. No worries—the whole file will be at the end of the chapter if you get lost. We also need a function to make jQuery work:

```
<script>
  $(function() {
    //replace with more code
  });
</script>
```

Let's start by setting up the dialog box. jQuery UI has the `dialog` (*http://bit.ly/jq-modal*) element, which takes care of many things for us, like creating a pop-up panel, positioning, and handling collisions.

Add the following inside the function you just created:

```
$( "#dialog" ).dialog({
    autoOpen: false,
    height: 500,
    width: 400,
    modal: true,
    dialogClass: 'book-dialog',
    show: {
      effect: "blind",
      duration: 400
    },
    hide: {
      effect: "blind",
      duration: 400
    }
});
```

There are a bunch of options here, and I encourage you to read the docs on jQuery UI (*https://jqueryui.com/*) as these little widgets can save you hours of trouble. It's mostly self-explanatory, and you may notice there are some cool animations you can do when showing and hiding the dialog.

Mousing Around

Now we will add functionality to the images that executes when a user mouses over them. Here is the code to add the mouseover functionality. It's a little convoluted, so look it over and then I will break it down:

```
$( ".selector" ).mouseover(function() {
    $( "#dialog" ).dialog({
      position: {
        my: "left top",
        of: this,
        collision: "flip"
      }
    });
    google.script.run.withSuccessHandler(function(ret){

      $( "#dialog" ).html('<p id="dialog-title">'+ret.title+'</p>'+
          '<hr>'+
```

```
'<div class="dialog-content"><img src="'+ret.imageUrl+'"
        height="200" width="150"></div>'+
'<div class="dialog-content">'+ret.description+'</div>'+
'<a href="'+ret.productPage+'" target="_blank">More info...</a>');
}).getImages(this.id);

$( "#dialog" ).dialog( "open" );
});
```

When we added the images to the table we gave them all the class="selector" attribute. Now we can add a mouseover event to all the elements in the selector class.

Each time the mouseover event happens we will run a function. We want the dialog to pop up close to the image that was moused over, so the first thing we want to do is set that position. We say we want it at the top left of this, which is the element from which the mouseover event was fired. Lastly, the collision setting means that if our dialog pops up off the page or collides with something, jQuery will adjust its placement for us.

Now that we have the box where we want it, we need to fill it with the right information. We need to pass the ID to our backend *Code.gs* so it will return the specific record.

Contacting the backend works like this:

```
google.script.run.withSuccessHandler(function(returnedValues){
    //do stuff in here
}).yourFunction(someArgument);
```

When we built the table and added the images, we used the id attribute to store the unique ID for each product. Because of this we know that the element that we used to trigger the event also holds the key to getting the correct information, and we can get that value by simply calling this.id.

Now we pass the unique ID in the server function argument as getImages(this.id). Remember, we are going to get back just one product from the server, and it is stored in the ret argument in the calling function. The whole thing looks a bit odd, so take the time to see how things flow here.

The content of the dialog box can be set as HTML—it's just a div, after all—so we will use jQuery to get the dialog box and the html method to add content. Because we already have all the information for the product saved in ret, we use the same technique we did in building the table earlier to create the different elements. You can get as fancy as you like here, but what I like to do is give things some CSS class or ID and work from the style section.

Everything is loaded for that specific product, and now all we need to do is show the dialog. Again, jQuery makes this a snap with $("#dialog").dialog("open").

Now that the dialog is open, we need to close it. Add this close call next:

```
$( "#dialog" ).mouseleave(function() {
  $( "#dialog" ).dialog( "close" );
});
```

This tells the app to close the dialog when the mouse leaves the dialog area. jQuery has also taken care of closing and opening if you mouse over a different element, even if you never move over and leave the dialog.

It's getting close now, and if you saved and loaded the dev version, it would actually work. However, there are some things that are not going to look right: for example, the dialog box is transparent, so your text gets lost in the page images. What we need now is some CSS magic.

After the closing `script` tag, add this style:

```css
<style>

.ui-dialog-titlebar-close{
    display: none;
}

.ui-dialog.book-dialog {
    font-family: Verdana,Arial,sans-serif;
    font-size: .8em;
    border-style:solid;
    border-width:1px;
    padding: 5px;
}

.ui-dialog{
    background: #F8F8F8;
}

#dialog-title {
  font-family: Verdana,Arial,sans-serif;
  font-size: 1.8em;
}

.dialog-content {
    width: 200px;
    float: left;
}

</style>
```

Save your work and reload the dev page. The images load as expected, but now when you hover over each image the dialog appears with the additional information, as shown in Figure 5-12. Moving off the image hides the dialog.

Figure 5-12. It's alive! The application has become interactive.

The application will now respond to the user, and the data is dynamically loaded for each product. Now that everything is working, you need to install the app in the Google Sites home page where you're storing the product pages. This is only a matter of installing the app as a script gadget, as we did in "Hello, Google Sites" on page 20. Figure 5-13 shows how your final project should look.

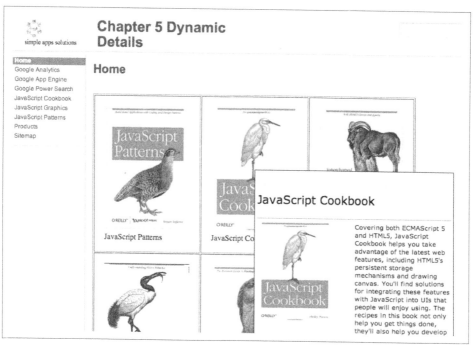

Figure 5-13. Final project installed in Google Sites

Delivering the Application

Your application is finished just in time to save the company from sliding into obscurity. With the new interactive interface, customers are throwing buckets of money into purchasing your products, and even Frank's boss is looking to promote you to a VP.

Those are all nice thoughts, but welcome back to reality. The application you have built certainly looks great, and it allows different styles from the CSS file, meaning a fresh look requires little work on your part. On the backend, the database is easy for anyone to use, allowing products to be added or removed with ease and product page templates to be generated automatically. It is a full system that is portable and can easily be set up for different product databases.

You have also learned some important techniques, such as loading data from or writing it to a spreadsheet, working with data objects and server calls, as well as applying CSS to elements. This knowledge will be useful as you progress to more advanced applications.

Up next, you will build an application that goes out into the world to find information and brings it back for a mashup that will keep you in the know.

Final Code

You can find all of the code for the files below on this book's Google Drive (*http://bit.ly/ ch5-final-code*).

Code for *index.html*:

```
<title>Chapter 5 Dynamic Details</title>
<? var data = getImages(); ?>
<? var j = 0;?>
<table cellpadding="20" border="1">
  <tr>
  <? for (var i = 0; i < data.length; i++) { ?>
      <?if(j==3){ ?>
          </tr><tr>
      <?   j=0
        }else{
          j++
        } ?>

      <td>
          <div><img id="<?=data[i].id?>" class="selector"
                  src="<?=data[i].imageUrl?>"
                  height="250" width="175"></div>
          <div class="book-titles"> <?= data[i].title ?></div>
      </td>
  <?} ?>
  </tr>
</table>
<div id="dialog"></div>

<script src="//ajax.googleapis.com/ajax/libs/jquery/1.9.1/jquery.min.js">
</script>
<script src="//ajax.googleapis.com/ajax/libs/jqueryui/1.10.3/jquery-ui.min.js">
</script>
<script>
  $(function() {

    $( "#dialog" ).dialog({
      autoOpen: false,
      height: 500,
      width: 400,
      modal: true,
      dialogClass: 'book-dialog',
      show: {
        effect: "blind",
        duration: 400
      },
      hide: {
        effect: "blind",
        duration: 400
      }
```

```
      });

    $( ".selector" ).mouseover(function() {
      $( "#dialog" ).dialog({
        position: {
          my: "left top",
          of: this,
          collision: "flip"
        }
      });
      google.script.run.withSuccessHandler(function(ret){

      $( "#dialog" ).html('<p id="dialog-title">'+ret.title+'</p>'+
            '<hr>'+
            '<div class="dialog-content"><img src="'+ret.imageUrl+'"
                        height="200" width="150"></div>'+
            '<div class="dialog-content">'+ret.description+'</div>'+
            '<a href="'+ret.productPage+'" target="_blank">More info...</a>');
      }).getImages(this.id);

      $( "#dialog" ).dialog( "open" );
    });

    $( "#dialog" ).mouseleave(function() {
      $( "#dialog" ).dialog( "close" );
    });
  });
</script>

<style>
.ui-dialog-titlebar-close{
    display: none;
}
.ui-dialog.book-dialog {
    font-family: Verdana,Arial,sans-serif;
    font-size: .8em;
    border-style:solid;
    border-width:1px;
    padding: 5px;
}

.ui-dialog{
    background: #F8F8F8;
}

#dialog-title {
  font-family: Verdana,Arial,sans-serif;
  font-size: 1.8em;
}

.dialog-content {
    width: 200px;
```

```
        float: left;
      }

      </style>
```

Code for *Code.gs*:

```
function doGet() {
  var html = HtmlService.createTemplateFromFile('index').evaluate()
       .setTitle('05 Dynamic Details')
       .setSandboxMode(HtmlService.SandboxMode.NATIVE);
  return html;
}

function getImages(id){
  var ss = SpreadsheetApp.openByUrl(
  'https://docs.google.com/a/simpleappssolutions.com/
  spreadsheet/ccc?key=0Aq1-C9ZFoxUmc&usp=drive_web#gid=0').getSheets()[0];
  var data = ObjApp.rangeToObjects(ss.getDataRange().getValues());
  if(id){
    for (var i in data){
      if(data[i].id == id){
        return data[i];
      }
    }
  }else{
    return data;
  }
}
```

CHAPTER 6

Automate Your Forms and Templates: A Web App for Drive

If your business is like most, it has forms lying around everywhere to get this process or that request done. Most of the time these forms are the same thing over and over, with a few things changed. Letters to say thank you for a purchase, patient intake, and filing with the court are all situations where we might encounter a form. Now I certainly would like to see everything in tidy data structures, but in reality we need forms to ground us in that paper, human-readable format—that is not going anywhere soon.

Google Apps gives us a great platform for collaboration, storage, and creation of documentation. However, there really is not a way to create forms that generates a nice, print-style page layout that is easy to distribute.

The Forms feature in Google Sheets is a great way to collect information; it uses a web page–style form that anyone who has ever used a computer can understand. This feature fills in a spreadsheet, making it a good tool for collection and analysis, but not for the output of a document, like your taxes. Another option is to build a template in Google Docs, leaving blank lines for where you would like certain things filled in. But what about extra instructions and the worry of a certain field getting missed? You could fire up Microsoft Word and spend the next week trying to get the form field insert function to work, and the next year explaining to users how to use it, but you know they will make copies on their hard drives that will come back to haunt you seven revisions later.

This chapter will go down a new road using Google Docs and Apps Script to form a system that takes a template and automatically generates a web form for your users to fill out.

What You Will Learn

You will learn how to:

- Edit Google Docs from a script
- Create new documents using the DocsList Service
- Work with template keys
- Generate a web form from text in a document

Supplies

You will need:

- A template document (created during the chapter)
- A script running as a web app

Application Overview

In this chapter, we will use the power of Google Apps Script to add functionality to Google Drive by building an application that will let you choose a template from your Drive folders and have the script automatically create a web form from key values you specify in the document. Not only will your web form be complete with instructions, but the script is smart enough to remove the instructions from the final copy. Filling out the form and submitting it will create a copy of the template, replace the template key fields with the answers on the form, and email the new copy back to you as a PDF. You can extend it to your whole company or even to the public, allowing for easy creation of common documents. The script is set up to generate a form for any template you provide it, so once it's set up, adding or changing forms is all done in Google Docs and no further coding is required.

Setting Up the Template

Templates come in every shape and size, and the information that needs to be replaced usually has some sort of key that tells you to replace it with your information. For example, if you've migrated over to Google Apps, there are documents produced by Google to help you tell your users what to expect, or to answer frequently asked questions. In these documents you will see red text in brackets that says things like "<your company name>". We will refer to these as *keys*, and they're how our script will figure out what gets replaced.

You can create keys any way you like, but for this book {%*Your Key*%} will be used. Therefore, if you would like to personalize the salutation, use Dear {%Recipient%}, in the form. There will also be a special instruction key that is used to display information to the user about what appears on the screen. Instructions look like this: {%Instruc tion:This is an automated template example.%}. When the script sees that a key starts with Instruction, it will know not to create a text box for user input and to remove that paragraph from the final document. The basic template is shown in Figure 6-1.

Welcome to making forms the easy way using Google Apps

{%Instruction:This is an automated template example.%}
Dear {%Your Name%},

This document is an example of what you may see in an online template. You can write templates right in the Google Docs editor using "keys" such as what you see above for your name. Collect several of your business process templates together in a Docs collection and use keys in the places you would like your staff to respond to questions. Special "Instruction" keys are used to add information to the form and will be removed in the viewer's copy of the document.

Once you have your templates ready, simply add a script gadget to your cooperate Google Sites page. The script builds a user interface and allows the viewer to choose a which template to use. Choosing a template will run a process that builds a web form using the keys in the selected template. The viewer fills out the web form and clicks submit creating a copy of the template with the keys replaced by the information they entered.
Your templates can contain all the rich formatting you love to use but without the trouble of buying special software or learning to use it.

Figure 6-1. The basic template

A template for this chapter with formatting is hosted on Google Docs (*http://bit.ly/ex-template*); click "File" and choose "Make a copy" to use the form.

If you can't access the document linked above, I've provided an example that will work fine in your own document.

If you have ever been a kid, you've likely filled out a Mad Lib. Let's give that a try in this template:

```
{%Instruction: Please fill in the words below for your Mad Lib example.%}

{%Exclamation%}! he said {%Adverb%} as he jumped into his convertible {%Noun%}
and {%Verb%} off with his {%Adjective%} wife.
```

```
{%Instruction:An exclamation is the act of exclaiming; outcry; loud complaint,
or protest. Examples include Ouch and Dang.%}

{%Instruction:A noun is the name of a person, place, or thing. Examples include
umbrella, sidewalk, telephone, and policeman.%}

{%Instruction:An adjective describes someone or something. Examples include cre-
ative, red, ugly, and short.%}

{%Instruction:A verb is an action word. Examples include run, jump, swim, and
fly.%}

{%Instruction:An adverb tells how something is done. It modifies a verb, and
usually ends in "ly." Examples include greedily, rapidly, modestly, and careful-
ly.%}
```

Make sure each instruction has its own paragraph, because the script will remove them.

You can use any formatting you like, and it will be carried over when the keys are replaced. This means you can have keys as document headers, in tables, and certainly in color, bold, italic, etc. Adding formatting really does give a polished look to the final document.

After you create your template, put it in a collection just for templates. This way, when you display a drop-down list for the user to choose from, he will only get templates, and not every other file in your Docs list.

Building the Script

Now that the form is ready to be filled out, it is time to build the script. Create a new script from the Drive menu, or copy the example script from "Hello Web App" on page 16. As usual, publish the script and, because we will again be working with objects, add the Object Service as shown in "Installing an Open Source Library" on page 60. The email function will need to get the user's information; because Google restricts access, you will want to choose the "Execute the app as the user" option.

Here is the doGet function in the *Code.gs* file:

```
function doGet() {
  var html = HtmlService.createTemplateFromFile('index').evaluate()
      .setTitle('06 Automating Forms')
      .setSandboxMode(HtmlService.SandboxMode.NATIVE);
  return html;
}
```

You will also want to open up the dev version so you can check your progress as we go along.

UI Setup

This will be a basic UI, with very few elements that you need to write in the code; however, the UI can fill itself with a hundred questions if that is what is in the template. The code does the work and makes you look like a coding genius.

This app is going to be running as you, and that means you need to create a folder in Drive that allows you to control access to the templates you want displayed in the UI. In Drive, create a folder called "Templates Folder." You will need the folder's ID, found in the URL of the address bar; this allows you to get the files from that folder. A specific folder gives you a place to create templates and update them as needed. The script will list all Google Docs in that collection, so it is best to think about it as being public. You can certainly restrict access to the documents there so they can't be edited, but your script will run as the user, and the user will need to be able to access your templates.

Now put your template file in the templates folder.

In the *Code.jg* file, you will need a global variable to hold the ID of your template collection. Add this line after the closing } of the doGet function:

```
var FOLDER_ID = '0B61-C9Nl4dO-SEhzOXA0SEZqMFU';
```

 Global variables are created outside of any function and can be accessed from anywhere in your script. You can update them as the script runs, but remember that when the UI is reloaded, they are set back to the original value.

You can test out the global variable by adding `<div><?=FOLDER_ID?></div>` to the *index.html* file and reloading the dev page. You will see the FOLDER_ID you stored in the global variable displayed in the web app.

Open the *index.html* file, and let's start laying out the page. The following code gives us a header to identify the app, several divs to hold the content, a section for scripts, and the page style. Note that the there is a body div that surrounds the other divs. This allows us to control how the app looks overall, such as adding some padding so that the text is not shoved all the way to the side of the screen:

```
<div class="body">
  <div><h2>This App will allow you to create a form from a template
  in Google Docs.</h2></div>
  <hr>

  <div id="options"></div>
  <div id="form-content"></div>

</div>
```

```
<script src="//ajax.googleapis.com/ajax/libs/jquery/1.9.1/jquery.min.js">
</script>
<script>
</script>

<style>
.body{
  padding: 10px;
}
</style>
```

 As of this writing, the Google Apps Script team has suggested that we not use the <body> tag, which is replaced by the Caja service during processing and may slow load times.

The next element to add is the listbox that will show the files in the templates folder. Because we only need to get the filenames and IDs, we can use the Google Apps Script scriptlets feature.

Here are the changes to the options div:

```
<div id="options">
  <?var files = DriveApp.getFolderById(FOLDER_ID).getFiles();?>
  <select id='template'>
    <option value="notSel">Select a Template</option>
    <?while (files.hasNext()){
    var file = files.next();?>
    <option value="<?=file.getId()?>"><?=file.getName()?></option>
    <?}?>
  </select>
</div>
```

First we get the files contained in the templates folder by accessing the DriveApp Service and using the folder ID. The getFiles method returns file objects for each file in the folder.

 It's not likely that you will have more than a few templates to load, but if you do have, say, hundreds, your app is going to become unresponsive waiting for Google to return all the files. A better option would be to put a "Loading Templates" indicator in the options div, and then do the processing by calling a backend function.

We don't want to add more stuff to the page than just what's required, so we will put the instruction to "Select a Template" right in the select box. Let's also give it the value notSel, so if the user selects "Select a Template," the event handler will simply clear the page.

Now we iterate the `files` object, getting the name and ID of each file and adding that to the `select` element's `option` tags. The `value` attribute is used to set the file ID, so that when the user makes a selection, that's the value used. This makes it easy for us to get the right template.

Pop over to the *Code.gs* file and click Run to grant access for Google Drive. If you don't do this, when you load the dev page you will get an "Authorization required" message. Load up the dev page and try out your listbox (Figure 6-2).

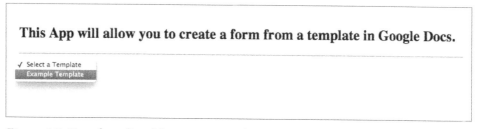

Figure 6-2. Templates listed from your Google Drive

 At the time of writing, the Docs Picker was not available in the HTML Service, but we hope to see it soon. This would allow you to replace the listbox with a button that opens the picker and creates more of a traditional file-choosing method.

Selecting the Template

When the user changes the value in the listbox, we want to go and get that template so we can build the form. To do this, we attach the jQuery `change` handler to the listbox.

This is done inside the `script` tags:

```
<script>
  $(function() {
    $( "#template" ).change(function() {
      //get the data here
    });
  });
</script>
```

The next step is to go get the template keys and build a form. We don't really need the whole template to build the form, as it only consists of the keys. Therefore, we will build the form in the *Code.gs* file on the server side, which will take care of all the details like getting the keys from the template and formatting the data. This means we will need to do some server-side communications using the `google.script.run` method.

Here is the whole code block for the change method. As always, we will go through it line by line

```
$( "#template" ).change(function() {
  if($('#template').val()=='notSel')return;
  $( "#form-content" ).append('<img src="http://goo.gl/23NPRI">
  Getting your form...');
  google.script.run.withSuccessHandler(function(ret){
    $( "#form-content" ).html(ret);
    $( "#templateForm" ).submit(processForm);
  }).buildForm($('#template').val());
});
```

Remember that we don't want the app to do anything if the user selects "Select a Template," so the first we're are going to run into is a check of the listbox value `$('#templa te').val()=='notSel'`. If this is `true` we return immediately, which gives the effect that nothing happened.

When we make calls to the backend or other services, it can take time to process the information, and if we don't provide some entertainment—like a loading indicator—the user may wonder if clicking the button did anything.

The next line will add a spinner *.gif* file, letting the user know something is going on. To make it disappear we replace the HTML in that div, so it is basically erased. You can use any image you like, but the animated style is most common (see Figure 6-3).

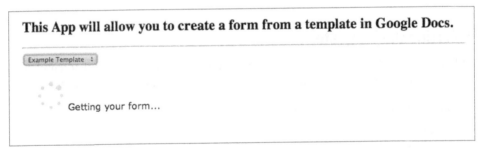

Figure 6-3. Entertain them!

The user has been stopped from making bad choices, and while she's distracted we will call on the backend for the data we need. The first part to run is the end of the statement, and the function we are going to call in the *Code.gs* file is `buildForm($('#templa te').val())`. `template` is the ID attribute of our drop-down list and, as you may remember, where we stored the template ID.

We will jump over to *Code.gs* and build that function in a minute, but first let's finish up here with what happens when the server returns:

```
$( "#form-content" ).html(ret);
$( "#templateForm" ).submit(processForm);
```

First, we set the `form-content` div HTML to what we get back from the server. Guess what? It's going to be a form and will have the `id` attribute `templateForm`. We want to be able to send the form back to the server after the user fills it out, and later we will create a function called `processForm`. We could have put that function right in the `submit` method, but I have reached my line-indent quota for the day. Joking aside, it's a good idea to move functions to their own objects—it makes your code more manageable.

Getting the Keys

When you write your templates, you want the template key to help users figure out what a field is when they are trying to fill it out. However, you also need that key value to represent a certain text-box name. Recalling the discussion in Chapter 5 on JavaScript-safe values, you know that `Your Email Address` will look good in the form but will cause an error as the `name` attribute of a text box. Conversely, `yourEmailAddress` is not, depending on the user, going to win you points with coworkers as they try to decrypt your form. Again, we will call on the ever-useful ObjApp to do some cameling for the attribute IDs when we start making text boxes.

We will need to get the keys several times in our app, so it makes sense to create a separate function to do this processing. The next function to add in *Code.gs* will return a set of keys in an array that looks like this: `[{text:'Key One', id:'keyOne'},{...}]`.

This is done by matching the key's unique identifiers (`{%Key%}`) and placing them into an array. At the same time, the key is cameled by the ObjApp Service, so that it can be used as a JavaScript name or ID.

Add the following function to your *Code.gs* file:

```
function createKeys(fileId){
  var templateTxt = DocumentApp.openById(fileId).getText();
  var templateVars = templateTxt.match(/\{\%[^\%]+\%\}/g);
  var keys = [];
  var oneEach = "";
  for (var i in templateVars) {
    var keyObject = {};
    keyObject.text = templateVars[i].replace(/\{\%|\%\}/g, '');
    keyObject.id = ObjApp.camelString(templateVars[i]);
    if (oneEach.match(keyObject.text) == null){
      keys.push(keyObject);
    }
    oneEach += " " + keyObject.text;
  }
  return keys;
}
```

When the user makes a selection, we will send the file ID in the argument `fileId`. This makes it easy to then use the `DocumentApp.openById` method to get the right template. We also use the `getText` method in this line to give us all of the text in one big, long string.

The template should contain keys that look like {%Key%}, so we now use the JavaScript `match` method to find all the keys. We only want one of each value, in case the template does something like ask for a person's name and uses the same key over and over. We don't want the form to render a text box for repeated keys; one will do just fine.

We return the keys variable when we are all done looking for keys in the text.

Generating the Form

In the section "Selecting the Template" on page 87, you created the change event handler to run a function called `buildForm`. Well, let's get that function built, so you can start seeing the web form generate.

Add the following function to your *Code.gs* file:

```
function buildForm(fileId){
  var keys = createKeys(fileId);
  if (keys.length == 0){
    return "Your selected template has no Keys";
  }
  var formHtml = '<form id="templateForm">';

  for (var i in keys) {
    var text = (keys[i].text);
    if(/^instruction/i.test(text)){
      formHtml+='<div>'+text.substring(text.indexOf(':')+1)+'</div>';
    }else{
      formHtml+= '<input type="text" name="'+keys[i].id+'" id="'+keys[i].id+'"
      placeholder="'+text+'"><br>';
    }
  }
  formHtml += '<input type="hidden" id="fileId" name="fileId" value="'+fileId+'">'
  formHtml += '<br><input type="submit" value="Create"></form>';
  return formHtml;
}
```

The first thing we do is pass that template file ID into the function and call up the `createKeys` function we created in the last section. This function returns an array containing the keys as text and their matching JavaScript-safe counterparts.

Now that the keys are ready to go, you can build the UI form. What looks like it might take hours to perform actually boils down to about seven lines of code, but it can make an endless number of fields to fill out.

After setting up the variable formHtml with the start of a form tag, start iterating through the keys array to build the instruction and input elements. To shorten up the typing, turn the current keys[i].text into a new string, text.

Before creating labels and text boxes, you need to find out if the template key is an instruction. When the template is created, you have the option of adding Instruc tion: to the beginning of a key. In the script, we use a regular expression to see if the key begins with Instruction: in both upper- and lowercase. If the test is true, we will only make a label, because instructions don't get answers.

 If your templates require other treatment, such as creating multiple-choice questions or formatting to highlight a section, you can simply add more tests and adjust the template. Try out a Section:Ti tle and add a background for the label using .setStyleAttri bute('background', '#A0A0A0').

You likely don't want the label to say "Instruction" at the beginning, so everything before and including the colon is stripped off using the substring method.

If no special test fits the key, then it must be a regular question, which gets the label/text box recipe.

When the text box is created, make sure to set the key's ID as the name of that box. Later this value will be read from e in the createDoc function for its value.

There are a few different ways to tell the user what a text box means, and in this case I chose to use the placeholder attribute.

After all the keys have been created, we are going to add one more hidden input where we will store the file ID. We do this because it's easy, and when we submit the form it will be passed along with the data and make it easy for us to retrieve it.

All that's left is a submit button, and you can return the form.

Test time! Save everything and reload the dev page. Now select a template from the listbox, and your template should be displayed as a series of instructions and text boxes (Figure 6-4).

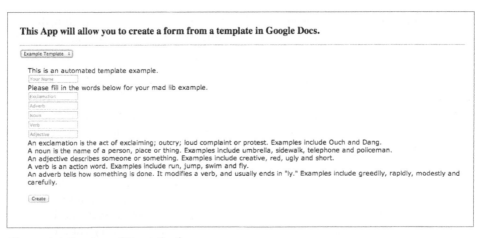

This App will allow you to create a form from a template in Google Docs.

Example Template ⊕

This is an automated template example.

Your Name

Please fill in the words below for your mad lib example.

Exclamation

Adverb

Noun

Verb

Adjective

An exclamation is the act of exclaiming; outcry; loud complaint or protest. Examples include Ouch and Dang.
A noun is the name of a person, place or thing. Examples include umbrella, sidewalk, telephone and policeman.
An adjective describes someone or something. Examples include creative, red, ugly and short.
A verb is an action word. Examples include run, jump, swim and fly.
An adverb tells how something is done. It modifies a verb, and usually ends in "ly." Examples include greedily, rapidly, modestly and carefully.

Create

Figure 6-4. Ready to fill out the form

Submitting the Completed Form

Heading back to the *index.html* file, we need to add the processForm function that was skipped over earlier.

Put the following code just inside the closing script tag:

```
function processForm() {
  $( "#form-content" ).append('<img src="http://goo.gl/23NPRI">
  Building your Document...');
  google.script.run.withSuccessHandler(function(formRet){
    $( "#form-content" ).html(formRet);
  }).createDoc(this);
};
```

If you look back in the code, you will see that this is the function that runs when the user clicks the submit button. Once again, it takes time to create documents, replace data, and send emails, which is why we have included more user entertainment.

Just like in the last section, where we got back an HTML form from the backend, this time we will get more HTML and add that to the form-content div.

Copying the Template and Adding Responses

The application is running great and rendering templates as web forms. Changing the file in the listbox will update the page with a new template. It may seem like we are only halfway done, but in reality it will only take one more function to wrap everything up.

Hopping back to the *Code.gs* file, the createDoc function is executed when the submit button is pressed and is the last function in the application.

Add the following function to *Code.gs*:

```
function createDoc(e){
  Logger.log(e.fileId)
  var keys = createKeys(e.fileId);
  var tempCopy = DriveApp.getFileById(e.fileId).makeCopy('copy'+ e.fileId);
  var doc = DocumentApp.openById(tempCopy.getId());
  var copy = doc.getActiveSection();
  for (var i in keys) {
     var text = keys[i].text;
     if(/^instruction/i.test(text)){
       if (copy.findText(keys[i].text) != null)
         copy.findText(keys[i].text).getElement().removeFromParent();
       }else{
         copy.replaceText('{%'+keys[i].text+'%}', e[keys[i].id]);
       }
     }
  doc.saveAndClose();
  var pdf = tempCopy.getAs("application/pdf");
  var bodyHtml = '<h3>Your document has been created and sent to your Email.
  </h3><br />';
  MailApp.sendEmail(Session.getEffectiveUser().getEmail(),
    'Your competed document', 'Your Doc is Attached',
    {attachments: pdf, htmlBody: bodyHtml, name: 'Drive Forms', noReply: true});
  tempCopy.setTrashed(true);
  return bodyHtml;
}
```

As you did when building the UI, get the keys again from the template. Now get the files in the templates folder.

We got the ID of the file from `fileId` and can now create a new document from the original template, in which we will replace the keys with the user's answers.

You need to get the active selection of the `tempCopy`, which at this time is the whole document. Now iterate over the keys. When a line of text starting with "Instruction" matches the regular expression in the `if` statement, that line is removed from the text string. The standard keys get replaced by the text values from the form using `e[keys[i].id]`, with the IDs for the keys used to name the text boxes?

That finishes creating the Google Doc and replacing the values; `findText` and `repla ceText` really make short work of it.

We want to email the final filled-out copy of the template back to the user as a PDF, and we do this with the `MailApp`. The file conversion is handled by the `tempCopy.getAs("ap plication/pdf")` method. Nice!

Click Run to take care of authorizations and reload the dev page.

Select a template, fill out the form, and click the submit button. In a few seconds you will get an HTML message that the email has been sent (Figure 6-5).

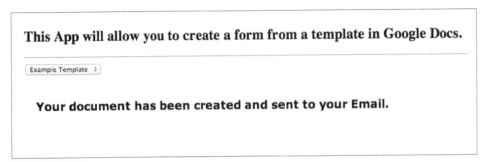

This App will allow you to create a form from a template in Google Docs.

Example Template ⁝

Your document has been created and sent to your Email.

Figure 6-5. The email has been sent—go have a look

Now go to your Gmail. If you have been using the provided template, you should get a chuckle from the Mad Lib. Figure 6-6 shows that the keys have been replaced and the instructions removed.

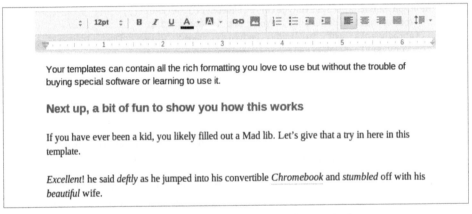

Figure 6-6. Document formatting stays intact after replacing the keys

Final Code

You can find all of the code for the files below on this book's Google Drive (*http://bit.ly/ code-ch6*).

Code for *Code.gs*.

```
function doGet() {
  var html = HtmlService.createTemplateFromFile('index').evaluate()
      .setTitle('06 Automating Forms')
      .setSandboxMode(HtmlService.SandboxMode.NATIVE);
  return html;
}

var FOLDER_ID = '0B61-C9Nl4dO-SEhzOXA0SEZqMFU';
```

```
function createKeys(fileId){
  var templateTxt = DocumentApp.openById(fileId).getText();
  var templateVars = templateTxt.match(/\{\%[^\%]+\%\}/g);
  var keys = [];
  var oneEach = "";
  for (var i in templateVars) {
    var keyObject = {};
    keyObject.text = templateVars[i].replace(/\{\%|\%\}/g, '');
    keyObject.id = ObjApp.camelString(templateVars[i]);
    if (oneEach.match(keyObject.text) == null){
      keys.push(keyObject);
    }
    oneEach += " " + keyObject.text;
  }
  return keys;
}

function buildForm(fileId){
  var keys = createKeys(fileId);
  if (keys.length == 0){
    return "Your selected template has no Keys";
  }
  var formHtml = '<form id="templateForm">';

  for (var i in keys) {
    var text = (keys[i].text);
    if(/^instruction/i.test(text)){
      formHtml+='<div>'+text.substring(text.indexOf(':')+1)+'</div>';
    }else{
      formHtml+= '<input type="text" name="'+keys[i].id+
      '" id="'+keys[i].id+'" placeholder="'+text+'"><br>';
    }
  }
  formHtml += '<input type="hidden" id="fileId" name="fileId" value="'+
  fileId+'">'
  formHtml += '<br><input type="submit" value="Create"></form>';
  return formHtml;
}

function createDoc(e){
  Logger.log(e.fileId)
  var keys = createKeys(e.fileId);
  var tempCopy = DriveApp.getFileById(e.fileId).makeCopy('copy'+ e.fileId);
  var doc = DocumentApp.openById(tempCopy.getId());
  var copy = doc.getActiveSection();
  for (var i in keys) {
    var text = keys[i].text;
    if(/^instruction/i.test(text)){
      if (copy.findText(keys[i].text) != null)
        copy.findText(keys[i].text).getElement().removeFromParent();
      }else{
```

```
                copy.replaceText('{%'+keys[i].text+'%}', e[keys[i].id]);
            }
        }
    doc.saveAndClose();
    var pdf = tempCopy.getAs("application/pdf");
    var bodyHtml = '<h3>Your document has been created and sent to your Email.
    </h3><br />
    MailApp.sendEmail(Session.getEffectiveUser().getEmail(),
      'Your completed document', 'Your Doc is Attached',
       {attachments: pdf, htmlBody: bodyHtml, name: 'Drive Forms', noReply: true});
    tempCopy.setTrashed(true);
    return bodyHtml;
}
```

Code for *index.html*.

```
<div class="body">
  <div><h2>This App will allow you to create a form from a template in Google
Docs.
  </h2></div>
  <hr>

  <div id="options">
    <?var files = DriveApp.getFolderById(FOLDER_ID).getFiles();?>
    <select id='template'>
      <option value="notSel">Select a Template</option>
      <?while (files.hasNext()){
      var file = files.next();?>
      <option value="<?=file.getId()?>"><?=file.getName()?></option>
      <?}?>
    </select>
  </div>
  <div id="form-content"></div>

</div>

<script      src="//ajax.googleapis.com/ajax/libs/jquery/1.9.1/jquery.min.js"></
script>
<script>
  $(function() {
    $( "#template" ).change(function() {
      if($('#template').val()=='notSel')return;
      $( "#form-content" ).append('<img src="http://goo.gl/23NPRI">
      Getting your form...');
      google.script.run.withSuccessHandler(function(ret){
        $( "#form-content" ).html(ret);
        $( "#templateForm" ).submit(processForm);
      }).buildForm($('#template').val());
    });
  });

  function processForm() {
    $( "#form-content" ).append('<img src="http://goo.gl/23NPRI">
```

```
      Building your Document...');
      google.script.run.withSuccessHandler(function(formRet){
        $( "#form-content" ).html(formRet);
      }).createDoc(this);
    };

</script>

<style>
.body{
  padding: 10px;
}

#form-content{
 padding:20px;
 font-family: Verdana, Geneva, "sans-serif";
}
</style>
```

CHAPTER 7

Collecting Data: A UiApp-Style Web App

It was a fine mess they had gotten themselves into. Scattered across the country, databases in various states of update and version, but not one location knew what the other was doing or if it could count on the "main hub" to have data that was less than a year out of date. That's when they called you.

You are the expert they place all their hope in, who can bring the worn and tired infrastructure back from the grave. As you gaze into the endless abyss of rot and decay from a thousand rickshaw contractors who went for a quick buck by adding another Band-Aid to the hemorrhaging artery, you realize that the days of the local copy are over—and you will be the one to usher in a new era.

The Installed App Has Died

Your coworkers will likely never know what goes into making a database work or the hardship of keeping it running. Fortunately, times are changing, and the days of building a frontend, installing it, maintaining it, and trying to keep everyone connected are rapidly coming to an end. The internal network has been replaced by the Internet, and cellular networks extend connections far beyond the reach of copper.

Today's databases are hosted in massive data centers that rarely fail to serve requests and cost almost nothing for storage. Frontend "installed" applications have been replaced by a browser, and connections are made globally. The data is always in sync because it is all in the same place, or appears to be, as the great hosts handle cross-data center transfers in milliseconds.

Why is this good for your database-building career? Simple: when you get ready to build your next database, you won't be thinking about servers and backups—those are covered by the host. Rather, your thoughts should fall on language support and how well your application will perform on the next generation of smartphones. Your rollout plan does not need to include installing software or worrying over the type of equipment it runs on, because if your client has a browser, it will run your software.

This chapter is about building a simple web-based database application. The entire application will be hosted within Google Drive using Fusion Tables and Google Apps Script. Because the user interface is hosted on the Web, changes you make are reflected in real time to everyone.

What You Will Learn

You will learn how to:

- Work with multiple panel views
- Use components
- Retrieve a specific record
- Work with Fusion Tables
- Create a basic database layout
- Use contextual buttons
- Generate OAuth and client authentication
- Use UrlFetchApp
- Automatically generate form fields
- Use Script Properties

Supplies

You will need:

- Google Fusion Tables
- Google Apps Script

Application Overview

This application will use the Google Apps Script web app–style UI and be sized to work well on smaller screens, like a phone or tablet, but not so small that it looks out of place when running as a gadget in a Google Site. When the application is loaded in the browser, the user will be presented with a welcome screen (see Figure 7-1) and options to search the records or create a new record.

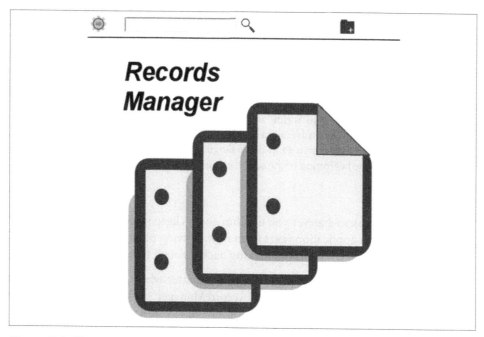

Figure 7-1. Users expect to see something when an application loads to let them know it's ready

Rather than the HTML Service used in most of this book, this chapter will focus on the UiApp Service, which is still alive and well in the Google Apps Script ecosystem. If you want a more extensive look at the UiApp Service, I encourage you to also pick up a copy of the first edition of this book, also available from O'Reilly.

Searching will connect to a Fusion Table that holds the records and returns the results as a table to the content area where the welcome image was displayed. There are mouse-over effects for the result rows, and clicking a result will open that record for viewing (with text fields disabled). An "Edit" button will also be added to the menu. Clicking "Edit" will unlock the fields, and the "Edit" button will be replaced with "Save" and "Cancel" buttons. "Cancel" resets the fields and goes back to "View Only" mode. Save writes changes to the Fusion Table. There will also be an "Insert" button that loads a blank form and an "Insert Record" button.

From the description you can guess that this is a typical database application, with the only real difference being the hosted web service and data storage. The model we use will be flexible in that no additional coding is needed to add or remove database fields; these changes are handled automatically from the Fusion Table. The script will also be portable, meaning that given a few key search fields, the script can be pointed at any Fusion Table and will work out of the box.

Setting Up

Big scripts, or applications, can consume thousands of lines of code, so having a plan is necessary to keep you organized. One of the first things you should create is a file to hold all of the items that will be used script-wide.

 In a Google Apps Script, any variables outside of a function will be global and accessible anywhere in the script. Best practice says that because JavaScript is a top-down language, any global variables should go at the beginning of the script, ensuring they will be available when called.

You can name your files whatever you like, but always keep in mind that you may need to come back to your application years from now. Leaving plenty of information about where things are will save you hours walking back through the code in the future.

Open up a new Google Apps Script; it does not matter where, because this will be a standalone application. Save the script as "Record Manager" and rename the "Code" file to "Settings." If you later decide that was not the name you wanted, it can be changed from the File menu without causing any problems in the script. Go ahead and delete the sample code; you won't be using that. The "Settings" file is a good place to keep things like button icons and any images you may want. We will be coming back here to add those soon.

Next, create a file called "CSS" where you will hold the style attributes for the whole script. You could also put your CSS objects into the "Settings" file, but having a dedicated file for CSS is handy and what most developers are used to. Copy in the applyCSS function:

```
function applyCSS_(element, style){
  for (var key in style){
    element.setStyleAttribute(key, style[key]);
  }
}
```

You might be wondering what the underscore before the arguments means. In Google Apps Script, to hide a function from the Run menu in the editor, you use an underscore. This can go a long way in cleaning up your Run menu options but is not otherwise needed.

Because there is nothing to apply CSS to yet, let's move on to the next file: doGet. Every UiApp needs an entry point, and the doGet function is your starting point in Google Apps Script UIs. Create a new file and name it "doGet," then add the create and return app statements:

```
function doGet(e) {
  var app = UiApp.createApplication().setTitle('Record Manager');
```

```
    return app;
  }
```

Publish the script with the settings of your choice and load a new tab with the published URL. You are now ready to start building the actual application—but first, a few words on design.

Building the Foundation

Honestly, I don't always know where a script is going until I've written a few hundred lines of code, but that can lead down some dark alleys, and you can waste time if you don't have a clear picture of where you need to go. A good way to stay on track is to sketch what you think the UI should look like and do. Google Drawings is a quick way to start working on the visual aspects, but you may also find the GUI Builder works very well and has the actual elements you will be working with.

Main Panel

Figure 7-2 shows the skeletal layout of the application. At the very bottom of the stack there will be a vertical panel to hold everything and give you a reference point to call on if you need access to certain elements.

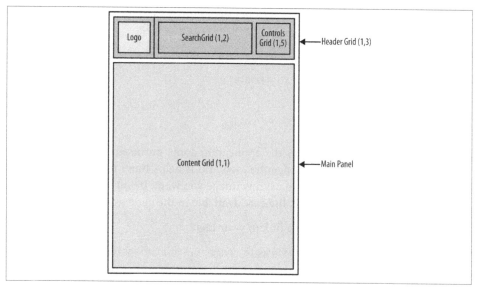

Figure 7-2. Drawing the application saves time and helps show you what will fit

Add the vertical panel to app, thus creating your application canvas:

```
var mainPanel = app.createVerticalPanel();
app.add(mainPanel);
```

Headers Grid

The topmost element in the application is a header that contains three areas: the logo, the search function, and buttons to control the application. These options will always be available to the user, but the context of the buttons will change depending on the current view. While there are only three areas, nesting widgets will give the application the flexibility it needs.

Add a one-row, three-column grid to the main panel:

```
var headerGrid = app.createGrid(1,3).setId('headerGrid').setWidth('500px');
mainPanel.add(headerGrid);
```

Setting the width here in the `headerGrid` means that this grid will set the width for the entire application and ensure the header goes all the way across. Don't forget to ID the grid: you might need to call on it later.

To add some separation from the rest of the elements, CSS will be used to put a border on the bottom of the table. This gives the effect of a horizontal line:

```
applyCSS_(headerGrid, _headerGrid);
```

Go back to the CSS file and add an entry for the CSS object `_headerGrid`. The example will have a simple look, like what is seen in other Google services, but if you would like more color, go ahead and add a background entry in the CSS:

```
var _headerGrid =
    {
    "border-bottom":"2px solid #404040"
    }
```

Branding

Branding is important, as it gives the application some grounding. When your users come to the application, they notice the logo and it helps them feel comfortable that they are in the right place. You can use any image you want. If you would like to use the images used to write this chapter, they are available in the code examples.

Go to the "Settings" file and add a link to your logo:

```
var logoImage = 'https://sites.google.com/site/scriptsexamples/scriptGear.png';
```

The reason you want to put the link here and not in the `doGet` code is to make it easier to reprovision the application. You only need to look in one place to change the icons and images. That organization will pay off.

In the "doGet" file, create a new image widget and set its size. This will keep things under control if the logo image is changed out:

```
var logo = app.createImage(logoImage).setSize('30px', '30px');
```

Note how the variable `logoImage` is accessed here even though it is not in the `doGet` function. The logo belongs in the upper-left corner of the header, which happens to be grid cell (0,0):

```
headerGrid.setWidget(0,0,logo);
```

Now that you have a few elements to look at, take a break and reload the published URL.

Search Component

The next part to add to the application is the record-search function. As with any search box, there will be a text box to type in the search words and a button to click that executes the search. Additionally, if the user hits the Enter key, the search should also be performed. These widgets and their handlers are a self-contained chunk of code that can be thought of as a *component*.

When building a complex application, finding ways to make components will save time and make the code easier to read. Think of it as having an engine ready to go for your car. The car won't go without the engine, and the engine can't run without input—gas—from the car's tank. Instead of putting all the parts of the engine in the car permanently, they are added as an engine component that can get swapped out for something with more power.

In Google Apps Script, it makes sense to store components in files of their own. Create a new file called "Search Component" and replace the default code with a new function:

```
function loadSearchBox(app) {

}
```

Note that the argument `app` is being passed into the function. This is done in order to build widgets from the current `app` object, which has not yet returned to the user.

 When the UiApp loads a page, it can't call on a handler. Therefore, you must pass the `UiApp` instance to any function that will be loading elements on the page. Calling `UiApp.getActiveApplication` within a function will not work because the original instance has not returned to the browser.

The best widget choice for this search component is a grid. This will allow plugging other widgets into the cells from anywhere in the script if needed. With a component, you don't return the `app` object, but rather the widget that was created. Again, this code could have been completely written in the doGet, so think of it as remotely creating the object (thinking back to using Java in Eclipse, there was a cool menu function that would move a chunk of code like this to a method):

```
var searchGrid = app.createGrid(1,3).setId('searchGrid');

return searchGrid;
```

Figure 7-3 shows the different parts that will need to go into building the component: there is a text box, and a button or an image if you like.

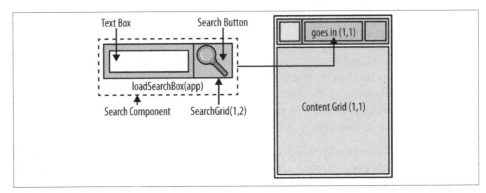

Figure 7-3. Components are sets of smaller parts that always go together and plug into the larger application

The text box goes in cell (0,0) of searchGrid and has a handler that fires on each keypress. Its function, searchView, will wait for keycode 13 (Enter key), and then load another component into the content grid (more on that just ahead):

```
var searchBox = app.createTextBox()
  searchBox.setName('searchBox')
    .setId('searchBox')
    .addKeyUpHandler(app.createServerKeyHandler('searchView')
    .addCallbackElement(searchBox));
searchGrid.setWidget(0,0, searchBox);
```

The text box name and ID are both set so that the value entered by the user can be passed through the handler in e.parameter. Pressing a key makes an entry when the button is pressed down, so a keyUpHandler will be used to ensure the input is captured. The callback is the text box itself, because that is the only thing we need to perform a search.

Most users will hit the Enter key after typing, but if there is not a way to tell the users what that text box does, they may become confused. The magnifying glass is a well-known icon for search, and a good choice if you would like to have an image. A button labeled Search is also effective, and less work to create.

Because we want this application to have a nice visual appeal, images designed by the author will be used for the buttons. You are free to use them in any of your applications. Switch over to the "Settings" file and add the search icon URL:

```
var searchIcon = 'https://sites.google.com/site/scriptsexamples/searchicon.png';
```

Now add the image to cell (0,1) of the searchGrid and add a clickHandler similar to the keyHandler on the text box. Don't forget to set the size, as it would be unfortunate to have a four-inch-tall magnifying glass:

```
var searchButton = app.createImage(searchIcon)
    .setSize('25px', '25px')
    .setId('searchButton')
    .addClickHandler(app.createServerClickHandler('searchView')
    .addCallbackElement(searchBox));
searchGrid.setWidget(0,1, searchButton);
```

In the "doGet" file, add a line to load the search component into the header grid:

```
headerGrid.setWidget(0,1, loadSearchBox(app)); //search component
```

Modular building can yield the benefit of knowing something works and moving on. Go ahead and reload the published page to see where you are. Typing in the box or clicking the button will cause an error because of the missing searchView function, but you should see that your component has loaded.

Navigation Component

Now that you have built one component, the next one will be a snap. The last cell in the headerGrid is for the buttons that allow a user to create a new record or edit and save existing records. Again, a grid is the best tool, because each button can be placed and replaced if necessary.

Create a new file named "Navigation Component" and add the code to create a grid six cells wide to accommodate all the buttons:

```
function loadNavigation(app) {
    var navPanel = app.createGrid(1,6).setId('navPanel');
    var newFileButton = app.createImage(newFileIcon)
        .setSize('25px', '25px')
        .setId('newFileButton')
        .addClickHandler(app.createServerClickHandler('viewRecord'));
    navPanel.setWidget(0,0, newFileButton);
    return navPanel;
}
```

For now there is just one button, but more will be dynamically added later, depending on the context of the application. Don't forget to add a link for the icon in "Settings:"

```
var newFileIcon =
'https://sites.google.com/site/scriptsexamples/newFileIcon.png';
```

The component is ready to be loaded into the header:

```
headerGrid.setWidget(0,2,loadNavigation(app)); //navigation component
```

Content Area

Now that the header is loaded, it is time to start thinking about the content. What the users see will depend on what they are doing in the application. For example, when loading the page, a welcome image should be the first thing they see. Next, they might search and get several records, where clicking a specific record shows just that record's details. These different states can be thought of as *views*. Therefore, a Search view will show search results, while a Record view may have many other views, such as Edit and View Only. These are all going to be displayed in the single-celled `contentGrid`.

You might be asking yourself, "Why only one cell?" The answer lies in the same concept used for the header: we can build components and swap them out in the same grid location to give the user many views in the same space. Another way to think of it is that when the Search button is clicked, the script builds a search results component and puts it in the content grid. Then, when the user wants a certain record, the script builds a record component and puts it in the same cell in the content grid—thus writing over the previous component.

 You can't use panels to switch out component views, because they only have add methods and no remove method. If you add a component to a panel and then add another component to the same panel, it will not overwrite the first component but rather get stacked on top of the first component. This is why a grid is used for creating application views by writing to the same cell.

Creating this magic view manager is simple—just add a 1×1 grid to the main panel:

```
var contentGrid = app.createGrid(1,1).setId('contentGrid').setWidth('100%');
mainPanel.add(contentGrid);
```

The ID is important, as you can imagine—we will be calling on this grid often—and setting the width to 100% ensures the area will be as wide as the application.

In this application, the users will always need to decide what to do first, so instead of having a big blank area, let's give them a splash screen.

Add an image link in "Settings:"

```
var startImage = 'https://sites.google.com/site/scriptsexamples/'+
                'RecordsKeeper.png';
```

Now create the image widget and load it in the `contentGrid`:

```
var splash = app.createImage(startImage).setSize('500px', '500px');
contentGrid.setWidget(0,0, splash);
```

That is the end of the doGet function and the shell of the application. Figure 7-1 displays your work up to this point. In the next section you will start pulling data from a Fusion Table and putting some content views into that shiny new space.

Search View

Now that there are some items to click, it's time to start wiring up actions and make the application come to life. The Search button is straightforward: click it and it sends the content of the textBox to your function. The textBox is a different story, because you want to know when the user is done entering text and is ready to search (signaled by hitting "Enter"). On each keypress, the key handler will execute the function, and this means you must look at the key that was pressed to see if it was the "Enter" key.

Loading the search into the content grid will be much like what was done in the header, where a component was used. This way the search can be swapped out with other types of views but without the need to change the page.

Start by creating a new file named "Search View" and a function named searchView, the name that was specified in the Search button and textBox handlers from the last section:

```
function searchView(e){
  var app = UiApp.getActiveApplication();
  return app;
}
```

The very first thing that must take place is to handle that keypress. Each time a key is pressed the function will run—not such a good idea unless you are trying to simulate Google Instant. The problem is that the user experience may not be great if the connection is slow and results don't display right after a keypress. We will not attempt instant results here, but if you are interested, the best way to go about it is to fetch the results that start with the first letter entered and keep them in an array. Then start providing results from the array after the third letter is entered.

For our application we need to know if it was the Search button or the textBox that executed; that is determined by e.parameter.source.

 The values passed by a handler carry some very important properties. e.parameter.source will tell you the ID of the widget that executed the handler so you know who is calling. e.parameter.key Code will tell you the keycode for a given key, which is how you find the Enter key (the Enter keycode is 13, by the way).

An if statement helps to figure out what to do given the event that comes into the function. If the Search button was clicked, we could just go ahead and run the function, but what if there was no value entered in the textBox? Later in this section you'll be able to figure out why this will return all the results in your database, which may not be desirable. To keep that from happening, check to see if the textBox has a value of nothing (not "null," that is different; a textBox with nothing entered has a value of ' ', also known as an empty string).

The next check is for the Enter key when the caller is also the textBox. If the conditions are true, the textBox empty, or the Search box was not sending the Enter key, then we just return the app. On the user's side of things, it looks like they are just typing in the box:

```
if (e.parameter.source=='searchBox' && e.parameter.keyCode!=13 ||
    e.parameter.searchBox=='') {
  return app;
}
```

After entering this code, try out the UI. Typing in the box, pressing "Enter," and clicking the Search button don't seem to do anything; that is because the app is being returned with no changes. There is no need to have an else part to the if statement; it is sufficient to just send back the call and wait on the next.

Once an acceptable condition has made it past the if gatekeeper, we can assume a list of matching data needs to be returned from the database. For this component you will build what is almost a mini app inside your application. Create a vertical panel to hold everything that will be returned and inserted in the content grid. You can set values in a widget already loaded in the UI using getElementById.

 Remember that getElementById is a one-way street; you can set values but you can't get them. The only way to get a value is to push it through a handler.

One way to understand this is to compare it to ordering at a restaurant. You figure out what you want on the menu and ask the waiter to get it. The waiter heads to the kitchen, gets a plate, and loads it with the food you asked for, then brings it back to the table for your consumption. We need to build the plate, along with something to keep the bread from soaking up all the gravy. When you need to add data to a UI, but you don't know how many items there will be, the right tool is a *Flex Table*. To give things some breathing room, set the cell padding at 5. Call this variable searchHeader because the user will need to know what the data returned means. This first Flex Table will contain the headers for the data that is returned by the search:

```
var searchPanel = app.createVerticalPanel();
app.getElementById('contentGrid').setWidget(0,0, searchPanel);
var searchHeader = app.createFlexTable().setCellPadding(5);
searchPanel.add(searchHeader);
applyCSS_(searchHeader, _headerGrid);
```

Notice that there is CSS applied to the header table. This is the same CSS used to put a line under the search component and gives a nice consistency. Searching from the UI will now replace the welcome graphic with a tiny underline where the empty table is.

After the headers comes the data, so make a second Flex Table to hold it and add it to the search panel. Because the search panel is a vertical panel, the two tables will line up nicely and appear to be the same table to the user:

```
var searchTable = app.createFlexTable().setId('searchTable');
searchPanel.add(searchTable);
```

Creating the Data Store

Now that we have a few tables, we need something to fill them, but we don't have a data store yet. For this application we are going to use a Google Fusion Table (*http://bit.ly/ g-fusion-t*). What is that? The short answer is that it is a flat, nonrelational database that can hold huge amounts of data. What makes it attractive is that it has many visualization tools built on top of it, allowing you to see your data in very creative ways. For example, the application we are building in this chapter could have a location column that allows a direct export to Google Maps, so you can see where your customers are being best served. Fusion Tables has an API, which is how we will connect to it. But what makes it a very interesting option for developers like you is that it uses SQL-style arguments to interact with the tables.

You can make a Fusion Table in Google Documents (*http://bit.ly/create-gtable*) right from the "Create" button ("Create"→"Table").

Click "New table" on the left and select "New empty table." You can change the name of the table (Edit→"Modify table info"), but what we are really interested in is the ID of the table. Look in the address bar and find the string after docid=; that number is your table ID.

The Fusion Tables API will allow you to control the table by adding or removing columns, setting the names and types of columns, and using all the data access features you would expect. While you have the new table open, let's change around some of the columns so it will be set up for the application we are building in this chapter.

Click "Edit," choose "Modify table info," and change the names and data types to match what you see in Figure 7-4.

If you make a mistake or need to delete or add a row, just go back to the Edit menu and find the choice to fix the problem.

Add a few rows of information to have something to work with while building the application. Once your columns are set up and a few records entered, make a note of the table ID and head back over to your script.

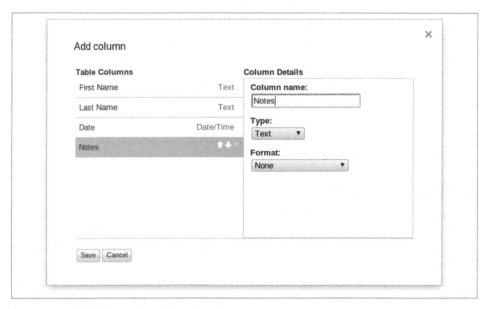

Figure 7-4. Modifying the table properties

Configuring Fusion Tables Access

I won't lie: Google has made this a constantly changing area that is a pain to set up. Always check the Google Docs on setup if you are seeing errors.

To begin, go to the Google Cloud Console (*http://bit.ly/cloud-console*) and click the Create Project button (Figure 7-5).

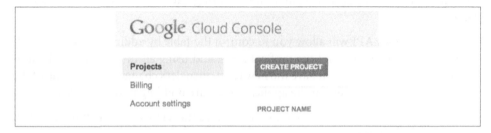

Figure 7-5. The new Cloud Console

After the project is created, you will need to click on "APIs & auth" on the left, and then "APIs." Go down the page until you find the Fusion Tables API and turn it on (Figure 7-6).

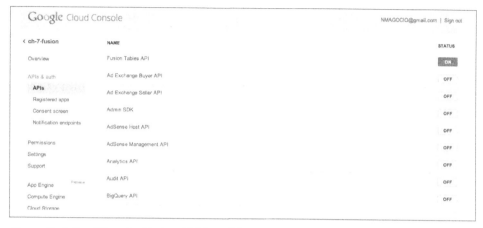

Figure 7-6. Enabling the Fusion Tables API

Now click on "Registered apps" and click "Service Account-project." This will open a screen that has a button to download the JSON (Figure 7-7). Download the file and open it in TextEdit or a similar program.

Figure 7-7. Getting your client secret

After opening the *.json* file you will need to locate your app's `client_secret` and `client_id` values.

Now you will need to add FusionTablesApp and ObjApp to your script resources. Here are the keys:

- `MTeYmpfWgqPbiBkVHnpgnM9kh30YExdAc`
- `MB8gYUxJO6QA4LYpjO7EWjeVJ5jnXUK_T`

Add the following code to your *Settings.gs* file. You will need to use your own values for the `FusionId`, `ClientId`, and `ClientSecret`:

```
function setup(){
  FusionTableApp.setFusionId('<YOUR_FUSION_TABLE_ID>');
  FusionTableApp.setClientId('443814946.apps.googleusercontent.com');
  FusionTableApp.setClientSecret('kXmuCqZJBuc19q3JAkL_P');
  Logger.log(FusionTableApp.getFusionHeaders());
}
```

If all has gone well, you should see a list of your headers in the log.

Getting Data from a Fusion Table

After the Search button is clicked or the Enter key pressed, the script will need to know the value of the `textBox`. In the "Search Component" file, the name of the `textBox` was set to `searchBox`, and it can be called from the value passed from the handler in `e.parameter`:

```
var searchKey = e.parameter.searchBox;
```

The Fusion Tables class has the method `searchFusion(target, where)`. The target specifies the columns you want to have returned in the search. Each value must be quoted. It can also take the all-columns argument, `*`. The only columns we want to search are the first and last names, so we can trim down the list. The second argument is a SQL `WHERE` statement, which completes the query by saying, "Where the column named First Name contains your search key, return matching records but only the values in columns First Name and Last Name":

```
var arrayResult1 = FusionTablesApp.searchFusion("'First Name', 'Last Name'",
  "'First Name'"+" CONTAINS IGNORING CASE '"+ searchKey+"'");
```

We want to search both the first and last name, but there is not an `OR` to the `WHERE` statement, meaning a second call must be made:

```
var arrayResult2 = FusionTablesApp.searchFusion("'First Name', 'Last Name'",
  "'Last Name'"+" CONTAINS IGNORING CASE '"+ searchKey+"'");
```

The `FusionTablesApp.searchFusion(target, where)` method returns an array `[[headers],[match row],[match row]…]`, which is perfect for turning into an object that we can then easily call on for values. The problem is that we need to combine them, and we only want the first set of headers located at [0] in each array. Taking care of this requires a few JavaScript tricks and the help of splice and concat:

```
arrayResult2.splice(0,1);
var concatArray = arrayResult1.concat(arrayResult2);
```

Splice off the first element in array number 2, and then glue the second array onto the first using concat. If you want to search more columns, just repeat the splice on each new array. Then, in concat, line up the arrays in the argument, as in (arrayResult2, arrayResult3, …).

The search array is put together and can be made into an object as follows:

```
var fusionSearch = ObjApp.rangeToObjects(concatArray);
```

As discussed in Chapter 5, rangeToObjects turns the header values into camelCase, so "First Name" becomes firstName. It also makes an object that can be used as fusion Search[0].firstName, to get the result to be the First Name value of the first result returned.

Figure 7-8 shows the relationships between the arrays and objects created in the last several steps.

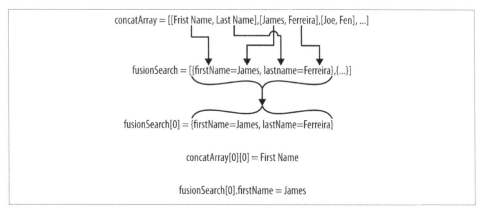

Figure 7-8. An example of an array converted to an object that uses key/value pairs

Loading the Data in the UI

The first element in the concatArray is an array of the column names, or the headers. When the search results are presented to the users they will need to know what the data is about, and having headers will accomplish the task. Set up a for loop and iterate the first element in the concatArray using its bracket call, [0].

The searchHeader table will hold the header values going across the page; therefore, when you iterate, set each header value into its cell by using parseInt(i) in the table column. Note that you don't have to know what information was in the search; the loop will take care of anything you hand to it.

Create a label widget to hold the value for each column, which is at [0][i]. Setting the width will help space things nicely across the application, but you may need to play with the value:

```
for (i in concatArray[0]){
    searchHeader.setWidget(0, parseInt(i), app.createLabel(concatArray[0][i])
                                        .setWidth('150px'));
}
```

A few important points: you could use setText in place of setWidget, which would make for less coding, but it would also mean that you have less control over setting style properties for the headers. What if you don't want to show certain columns? My question would be, "Why get them in the first place?" However, you might have a use case: let's look at that now. Load the UI in the browser, type in a few letters that exist in one of the records you added earlier, and see what you get. Figure 7-9 shows that the headers have been returned from the Fusion Table, telling us that everything is working up to this point and that there is an extra column, rowid, that we didn't ask for.

Figure 7-9. Sample headers returned from the Fusion Table

In a Fusion Table each row has a unique ID, and this is the only way to update a specific record. Therefore, having the row ID in your search results is important to working with a record—but you might not want to show it to the user. To hide it from view, it needs to not load into the header table. Before the table loads a header value, inspect it to see if it has the name rowid; if it does, use the continue statement to have the loop skip to the next value:

```
if (concatArray[0][i]=='rowid')
    continue;
```

Now when you reload the page, it will only show the First and Last Name columns. To hide more columns, add || (OR) statements to the loop conditions.

One reason for using the Fusion Tables class is that it adds the row id, which is not returned in a typical Fusion request. This simplifies working with the data.

The next step is to iterate through the results in the `fusionSearch` array and list out the values under each column. This could be done by simply adding the results into each row of the `searchTable`; however, the user should be able to click anywhere on the row and have that record open. If you add each value one at a time, you will also need to attach a click handler to each one. In the next section you'll see is a trick for highlighting the whole row that makes the upcoming solution even more attractive.

Remember that a handler can be added to most widgets, and the Flex Table will allow a click handler. We are going add a Flex Table to each row of the `fusionSearch` table, add a handler, and then fill the table in each row with the search results. Figure 7-10 shows the layout of tables in relation to the data they will hold.

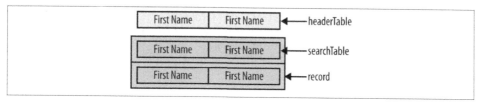

Figure 7-10. Example of Flex Tables within Flex Tables

For each element in the `fusionSearch` array, a new `record` table is created and a handler attached, so that clicking anywhere in that row executes the `viewRecord` function. Most importantly, each `record` table that is created will have an ID set to the `rowid` of the corresponding record that was returned in the search. When `viewRecord` runs, it will look at `e.parameter.source` to see who called it, and this is how we will know which record was selected:

```
for(j in fusionSearch){
  var record = app.createFlexTable().setId(fusionSearch[j].rowid)
     .setCellPadding(5)
     .addClickHandler(app.createServerClickHandler('viewRecord'));
  applyCSS_(record, _rows);

  //load record here

  searchTable.setWidget(parseInt(j), 0, record);
}
```

Additionally, CSS is applied to each row to add a line that separates each record. Don't forget to add a CSS entry in your "CSS" file:

```
var _rows =
    {
    "border-bottom":"2px solid #C0C0C0"
    }
```

Find the comment in the code that reads //load record here, and replace it with a loop to iterate the search results. This is done by iterating the number of headers in concatArray[0] as shown, giving "i" number of columns and also using the row in fusionSearch[j]. To ensure the right value goes in the correct column, use camel String(concatArray[0][i]). Written in English, this would read, "Get the first header name and camel it, then find the matching value in the current row of data from the search results":

```
for (i in concatArray[0]){
  if (arrayResult1[0][i]=='rowid')
    continue;

  record.setWidget(parseInt(j), parseInt(i),
        app.createLabel(fusionSearch[j][ObjApp
                       .camelString(concatArray[0][i])])
                       .setWidth('150px')
                //client handlers go here
                       );
}
```

Again, the rowid is skipped over to hide it from the user.

At this point you can load the UI page, do a search, and see results. Clicking a row will throw an error, reminding you to create the add viewRecord function. There is something else amiss as well.

Adding Client-Side Handlers

When you move the mouse over one of the records nothing happens, so the users won't know if the item is selectable or even if they are hovering in the right place. The best way to give them feedback is to add a few mouse handlers to each record that will change the display. You might be wondering why we are adding these handlers to each label and not to the Flex Table. The answer is that the Flex Table will not take a mouse handler, so we need a trick.

Unlike a standard handler that requires a trip to the server and back, the client-side handlers run from the browser, giving a very fast response time. When the user rolls over one of the labels, the client handler will find the record with the right ID and change its text and background colors. Rolling off sets them back to the way they were. Now the user has positive feedback for the record she would like to select:

```
.addMouseOverHandler(app.createClientHandler()
  .forTargets(app.getElementById(fusionSearch[j].rowid))
    .setStyleAttribute('color', 'blue')
    .setStyleAttribute('background', 'FFFF99'))
.addMouseOutHandler(app.createClientHandler()
  .forTargets(app.getElementById(fusionSearch[j].rowid))
    .setStyleAttribute('color', 'black')
    .setStyleAttribute('background', 'transparent'))
```

Viewing a Record

The user can search for records in the database; the next step is to focus on one record to view all of the details. The process is very similar to displaying the search results, but the columns will be listed down the page with a label on the left and a text box on the right. Later, certain headers will be picked out to allow special formatting, like a bigger box for the Notes field.

Figure 7-11 shows an example of how the layout will look using the columns in the example; however, the columns will be automatically generated to allow for changes in the database without the need to hardcode what will display.

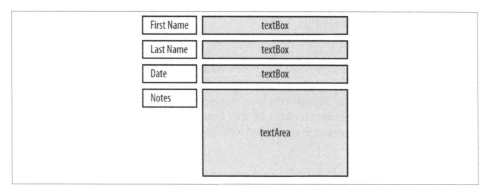

Figure 7-11. Layout of form elements

The record view will replace the search results in the content screen; therefore, it can be thought of as a component similar to the others.

Fetching the Correct Record

Create a new file, name it "Record View," and start off with the component code as before:

```
function viewRecord(e) {
  var app = UiApp.getActiveApplication();
  //add code here
```

```
    return app;
}
```

If you remember the last section, each row in the searchTable was given the ID of the rowid from which the record came. This allows us to use e.parameter.source to find out the name of the called record. It's handy that the caller is the record ID that we need to display. Load the ID into a variable to make the code more readable, and use the searchFusion method to call on a specific record:

```
var recordId = e.parameter.source;
var arrayResult = FusionTablesApp.searchFusion("*", "'rowid' = '"recordId"'");
var fusionRecord = ObjApp.rangeToObjects(arrayResult)[0];
```

The arguments say that we want all ("*") columns where the rowid is equal to the recordId variable. Because each row in a Fusion Table has a unique ID, there will be only one result. Next, the values need to be paired with each column using the rangeToObjects method. This returns an array even though it is only one element long. To save some writing, trim down the array to a single object using [0].

Now the correct record has been retrieved and the values loaded into a workable format. To create the UI, we need a Flex Table to fill with the content from the database:

```
var viewRecordTable = app.createFlexTable().setCellPadding(5)
.setId('viewRecordTable');
app.getElementById('contentGrid').setWidget(0,0, viewRecordTable);
```

 Unless you have some tricky arrangement for the panels and widgets, it's a good idea to get into the habit of adding them to their parent right after creating them. Even though we added the viewRecordTable to the contentGrid right after creating it, the table can be modified and more elements added to it later in the code.

The arrayResult[0] holds the column names from the database; for example, [First Name, Last Name, Date, Notes, rowid]. Don't forget that the searchFusion method always adds the rowid. To fill the viewRecordTable with content, iterate the values in arrayResult[0]. As discussed in Chapter 5, the elements are arranged three across the page and in rows continuing down the page for as much content as the database contains. If that is the look you are going for, a few more loops should get you there. We'll discuss getting a specific look or arrangement in the next section.

There are two elements that need to be created: a label for the name of the column and a textBox to hold the value. The first element in the setWidget method will specify the row in the Flex Table, and you must use parseInt(i) to ensure that it has been turned into an integer. Flex Tables are zero-based, so to put the label in the far left column, use the 0 argument for placing the label. Put the textBox right next to the label, in position 1:

```
for (var i in arrayResult[0]){

    viewRecordTable.setWidget(parseInt(i), 0,
                            app.createLabel(arrayResult[0][i]));
    viewRecordTable.setWidget(parseInt(i), 1, app.createTextBox()
                    .setId(ObjApp.camelString(arrayResult[0][i]))
                    .setName(ObjApp.camelString(arrayResult[0][i]))
                    .setValue(fusionRecord[ObjApp
                    .camelString(arrayResult[0][i])])
                    .setWidth('350px').setEnabled(false)
                );
}
```

Use `arrayResult[0][i]` to get the column's name and create the label. For the `text Box`, we want the ID and name values to both be cameled text of the column names.

Widget name and ID values must be JavaScript-safe, or they will throw errors. The `ObjApp.camelString` method will make the conversion for you.

The value for the column is held in `fusionRecord.<columnName>`. To ensure you get the right value for the right column, call on the current column name being iterated and camel it.

A little increase on the width gives a better presentation, and the `textBox` is set to disabled. The reason we set the `textBox` to disabled is to provide a View Only mode in the application. We don't want any changes unless they are intended, right?

Reload the UI page, do a search, and click one of the records. Figure 7-12 shows a specific record displayed in the content area, organized by rows.

	fe
First Name	James
Last Name	Ferreira
Date	10/27/11
Notes	Finish Chapter 7
rowid	201

Figure 7-12. View Only mode disables the text boxes to prevent unintended editing

Custom Formatting

Having all the details show up for the correct record is a great first step, but what if you need to hide something or make certain areas different than others? The `rowid` is not something your user will care about, and that Notes field is too small to read longer entries. To solve these issues, we will need to create a way to check if a certain column is going to be loaded and perform the appropriate action.

One way to check the column is with an `if/else if` statement. Managing this gets messy, though, and it's not very efficient because each `if` statement must be evaluated before going on to the next. This would not be a problem for our small database, but if your application was deployed in research the number of columns could go into the thousands, and that may make for a sluggish response.

In JavaScript, a better way to handle selecting specific criteria is to use a `switch` statement. A `switch` works by giving it a value and matching that value to a certain case you define (an optional default case will match if no cases fit the criteria).

Inside the `for` loop, modify the code to be set up as the default case. The value for the `switch` to evaluate is the column value. There's no need to camel it, as each case can take a string value as its argument:

```
switch (arrayResult[0][i]){

    //add more cases here

    default:
      viewRecordTable.setWidget(parseInt(i), 0,
                        app.createLabel(arrayResult[0][i]));
      viewRecordTable.setWidget(parseInt(i), 1, app.createTextBox()
                        .setId(ObjApp.camelString(arrayResult[0][i]))
                        .setName(ObjApp.camelString(arrayResult[0][i]))
                        .setValue(fusionRecord[ObjApp
                        .camelString(arrayResult[0][i])])
                        .setWidth('350px').setEnabled(false)
                        );
      break;
}
```

To get started, the Notes section needs to be a text area, not a box. This will give the user a larger area for display and scroll bars if the text goes beyond the size settings.

Insert the Notes case above the default case:

```
case 'Notes':
  viewRecordTable.setWidget(parseInt(i), 0,
                    app.createLabel(arrayResult[0][i]));
  viewRecordTable.setWidget(parseInt(i), 1, app.createTextArea()
                    .setSize('350px', '100px')
                    .setId(ObjApp.camelString(arrayResult[0][i]))
```

```
                                    .setName(ObjApp.camelString(arrayResult[0][i]))
                                    .setValue(fusionRecord[ObjApp
                                    .camelString(arrayResult[0][i])])
                                    .setEnabled(false)
                                );
            break;
```

Each case starts with the column name as a quoted string and ends with break;. Change the textBox to a textArea (.createTextArea()) and use setSize to give the box some boundaries.

The rowid, while very important to the application, has no meaning to the user. Set a case for it next, and hide it by setting its visibility to false. Why load it at all? We will get to that when saving changes (think e.parameter):

```
        case 'rowid':
          //no label required
          viewRecordTable.setWidget(parseInt(i), 1, app.createTextBox()
                                    .setId(ObjApp.camelString(arrayResult[0][i]))
                                    .setName(ObjApp.camelString(arrayResult[0][i]))
                                    .setValue(fusionRecord[ObjApp
                                    .camelString(arrayResult[0][i])])
                                    .setVisible(false) //hide the row
                                );
          break;
```

Formatting a listBox

So far this application has displayed text, but it would be useful to have the user make a selection from a predefined list. The listBox is the widget that displays as a drop-down box with selections to choose from; it can be created just like a text box, but a few more steps are needed to set up the options.

Open your "Settings" file and create an array with the options you would like to appear in the list:

```
        var statusValues = ['Open', 'Pending', 'Closed'];
```

Next, open the Fusion Table and add a new Status column: click "Edit," choose "Add column," type in "Status" as the column name, and use the arrow icon to move it above the Notes column, as shown in Figure 7-13.

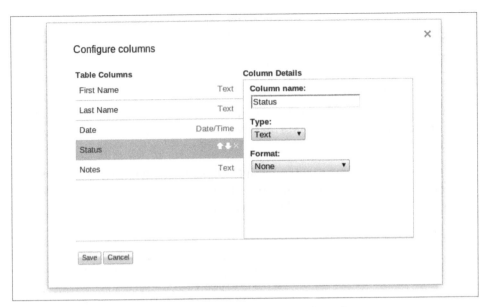

Figure 7-13. The format of the column is set in the type drop-down

If you reloaded the UI page now, you would see that the new Status column has been generated as a text box.

The Status case is similar to the other cases, but it has additional code to add values to the listBox from the array in the "Settings" file:

```
case 'Status':
  viewRecordTable.setWidget(parseInt(i), 0,
              app.createLabel(arrayResult[0][i]));
  var status = app.createListBox()
              .setId(ObjApp.camelString(arrayResult[0][i]))
              .setName(ObjApp.camelString(arrayResult[0][i]))
              .addItem(fusionRecord[ObjApp
              .camelString(arrayResult[0][i])])
              .setWidth('100px').setEnabled(true);
  viewRecordTable.setWidget(parseInt(i), 1, status);

  for (k in statusValues){
    if (statusValues[k] != fusionRecord[ObjApp
                            .camelString(arrayResult[0][i])])
    status.addItem(statusValues[k]);
  }
  break;
```

For a new record, the Status column will be an empty string and will render as a blank box with a down arrow. That will be fine for this application, but if you need to present more information to the user, simply add an if statement before the listBox is created to handle empty strings.

After creating the listBox, the for loop loads in the options from the array and includes a check for an existing value, so it is not displayed twice in the list. Note in the preceding code that the listBox is enabled so you can click on it. Don't bother disabling it, because a variable will be added in "Inserting a New Record" on page 128 to control that.

Reload the UI page and go through the steps to set up a record. Now click the Status listBox and choose an option.

Editing a Record

Things are looking good. The user has an application that opens with a nice greeting, searches the database when keywords are entered, and displays specific records. We did not want to allow a record to be changed while viewing to avoid inadvertent changes, but now the functionality will be added to make edits. This is actually very easy to do: simply enable the textBoxes. However, there will need to be a button and method to perform the task.

Open the "Settings" file and add an Edit icon:

```
var editIcon = 'https://sites.google.com/site/scriptsexamples/editIcon.png';
```

An Edit button is created before the return app; line and placed in position (0,1) of the navPanel. It will call on the editRecord function, yet to be created, and pass the viewRecordTable in the callback:

```
var editButton = app.createImage(editIcon)
    .setVisible(true)
    .setSize('25px', '25px')
    .setId('editButton')
    .addClickHandler(app.createServerClickHandler('editRecord')
                    .addCallbackElement(viewRecordTable));
app.getElementById('navPanel').setWidget(0, 1, editButton);
```

Create a new file and name it "Edit Record." Write the editRecord function, shown next, and get/return the active application.

The Fusion Tables class (*http://bit.ly/fusion-t-ex*) has the getFusionHeaders method, which returns an array of all the column names. Use camelArray on this and you will have an array of column names that match the textBox names. Iterate the headers and set each matching element to enabled:

```
function editRecord(e){
  var app = UiApp.getActiveApplication();

  var headers = ObjApp.camelArray(getFusionHeaders());

  for (i in headers){
    app.getElementById(headers[i]).setEnabled(true);
  }
```

```
    app.getElementById('editButton').setVisible(false);
    app.getElementById('newFileButton').setVisible(false);

    return app;
}
```

During Edit mode, you don't want the user to create a new record; you are already editing, so hide these buttons by setting their visibility.

Save your work and reload the UI. The Edit button will appear when a record is loaded in View Only mode, and clicking Edit will enable all the textBoxes.

There are two outcomes to editing a record: save the changes, or cancel, which does not save changes. Let's deal with cancel first.

Open the "View Record" file and add a Cancel button after the Edit button. The visibility is set to false, so the Cancel button is not seen when the view is loaded. The function it calls will be viewRecord. That is interesting because viewRecord was what loaded the View Only mode. What we are doing here is reloading the view for the same record without making changes, giving the appearance that the data was reset in the application:

```
var cancelButton = app.createImage(cancelIcon)
    .setVisible(false)
    .setSize('25px', '25px')
    .setId('cancelButton')
    .addClickHandler(app.createServerClickHandler('viewRecord')
                        .addCallbackElement(viewRecordTable));
app.getElementById('navPanel').setWidget(0, 3, cancelButton);
```

Don't forget to add a Cancel icon in the "Settings" file:

```
var cancelIcon = 'https://sites.google.com/site/scriptsexamples/CancelIcon.png';
```

To make the button show up in the navigation, add a line at the end of the "Edit Record" file to make it visible:

```
app.getElementById('cancelButton').setVisible(true);
```

If you tried the Cancel button now it would give you an error, because when viewRe cord runs it uses the name of the caller to find the record. Coming from the search, the name is a rowid, but coming from the Cancel button, the name is e.parameter.source = cancelButton. At first this appears to be a huge problem, but remember that view RecordTable was passed in the cancel handler and that e.parameter.rowid holds the rowid value. See why we just hid it earlier?

To make the Cancel button work, modify the beginning of the "View Record" file to check e.parameter.source by replacing the line:

```
var recordId = e.parameter.source;
```

with an if/else statement to check if the Cancel button was clicked:

```
if (e.parameter.source == 'cancelButton'){
  var recordId = e.parameter.rowid;
  app.getElementById('newFileButton').setVisible(true);
}else{
  var recordId = e.parameter.source;
}
```

Reload the UI page and check the operation. When changes like deleting content are made, clicking Cancel resets the record and places the user back in View Only mode.

Saving Changes

When the user makes changes, they will need to be written to the spreadsheet. First, create a Save button. As with the Cancel button, an icon is added to the navigation panel.

 In this chapter, icons have been used for the buttons to create a custom look and feel. However, if you don't have the time for this or don't care to take the time for this, you can use a button widget. By using CSS to style all the buttons, you can add a creative flair with rounded corners and other effects.

In the "Settings" file, add a Save icon:

```
var saveIcon = 'https://sites.google.com/site/scriptsexamples/saveicon.png';
```

Insert the Save button in the "Record View" file after the Cancel button, so it can join its friends in the navPanel at location (0,2). The arrangement between the buttons is not really important—just don't put two buttons in the same cell, or only the second one set will show, making for a great deal of confusion and troubleshooting. The handler will execute the saveRecord function (which we'll create in a moment) and, like the Cancel button, it adds the viewRecordTable as the callback, giving access to all the widgets contained in the table:

```
var saveButton = app.createImage(saveIcon)
    .setVisible(false)
    .setSize('25px', '25px')
    .setId('saveButton')
    .addClickHandler(app.createServerClickHandler('saveRecord')
                .addCallbackElement(viewRecordTable));
app.getElementById('navPanel').setWidget(0,2, saveButton);
```

You will need to change the visibility of the "Save" button in the "Edit Record" file when the edit view is loaded by adding one more line before returning the app:

```
app.getElementById('saveButton').setVisible(true);
```

The buttons are now in order, and the Save Record file can be created to handle saving to the Fusion Table. What it takes to save to the Fusion Table may surprise you:

```
function saveRecord(e){
  var app = UiApp.getActiveApplication();

  FusionTablesApp.writeFusionObj(e.parameter);

  return app;
}
```

I'm joking: it is only one line of code. The reason is that the Fusion Tables class method, `writeFusionObj`, uses the values in `e.parameter` to determine which row needs to be written to and the correct values for each column.

The user should be notified that the changes were saved, and the best way to do that is the "Last look" scenario: send the user back to the View Only mode after the save, where he can check that the values are correct before leaving.

The values are already there in the `textBoxes`, so disable them and update the visibility of the buttons:

```
for (i in headers){
    app.getElementById(headers[i]).setEnabled(false);
}

app.getElementById('cancelButton').setVisible(false);
app.getElementById('saveButton').setVisible(false);
app.getElementById('newFileButton').setVisible(true);
app.getElementById('editButton').setVisible(true);
```

Inserting a New Record

It may have seemed strange to wait until so late in the application development to start creating new records, but this is because inserting a record piggybacks on the work that is already done, and there is no need to add any new files.

The "New File" button has been hanging around in the navigation bar forever, so it is time to put it to work. Looking back to the "Navigation Component" file where the button was first created, you will note that it executes the `viewRecord` function. If you are having déjà vu, don't worry, you ran into the same problem with the Cancel button.

Open the "Record View" file and get ready to make a few changes. When `viewRecord` runs, all the `textBoxes` are disabled, and that would mean an extra click to start entering data. To overcome this limitation, create a variable for enabled status right after the app is created, and replace the three `false` values in the `setEnabled` calls to `newRecord`. Right now that will have the exact same effect, but it gives us the option to toggle `newRecord` to `true` and have all the `textBoxes` live when loading `viewRecord`:

```
var newRecord = false;
```

Reading down the code, skip past the `if` statement for the Cancel button and create a new `if` statement to handle the `newFileButton`. The `e.parameter.source` will tell us that the caller is the `newFileButton`. The idea is to create an object that is the same as what would be created by running a search for a specific ID, but with empty values. Grab the column names with the `getFusionHeaders` method. You will need to add `rowid` by pushing it into the `arrayHeaders`. To work in the rest of the code, `arrayHeaders` needs to be enclosed in brackets and set as the value for `arrayResult`. The `fusionRe` cord can be an empty object because we don't want any values. This is a new record, so set `newRecord = true`.

To preserve the previous function, add an `else` statement and enclose the two lines that created the data variables:

```
if (e.parameter.source == 'newFileButton'){
  var arrayheaders = FusionTablesApp.getFusionHeaders();
  arrayheaders.push('rowid');
  var arrayResult = [arrayheaders]
  var fusionRecord = new Object();
  newRecord = true;
}else{
  var arrayResult = FusionTablesApp.searchFusion("*", "'rowid' = '"+
  recordId+"'");
  var fusionRecord = ObjApp.rangeToObjects(arrayResult)[0];
}
```

Because the UI is going to load with the `textBoxes` enabled, there is no need for the "Edit" button to be showing. To hide it, go to the end of the code before the app returns and add an `if` statement to check for the `newRecord` value and hide the Edit button if it's `true`:

```
if(newRecord)
  editButton.setVisible(false);
```

Reloading the UI page and clicking the Create Record button will now load the form, ready to accept values as shown in Figure 7-14.

Inserting a record in a Fusion Table is not the same call as saving a record, and requires a different method. Currently there is no value in the `rowid`, which could be detected from a Save button press; however, to add some distinction for the user, an Insert Record button will be used.

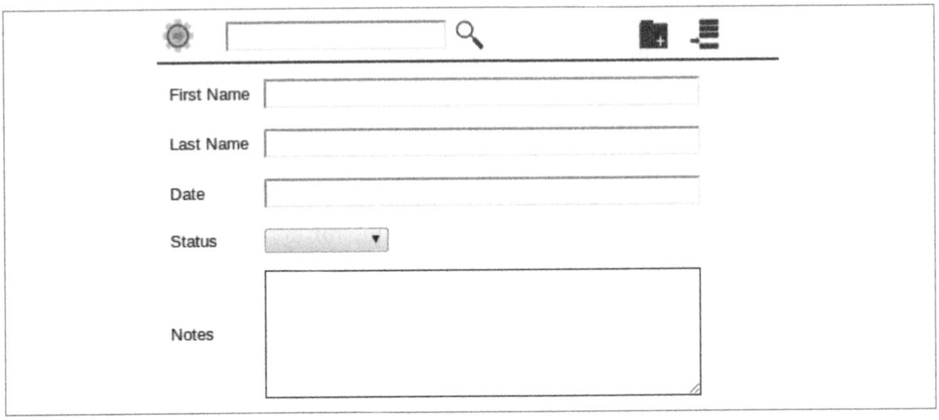

Figure 7-14. The Create Record form is the same as the Edit form, but no record has been inserted

You know the drill; add an icon in the "Settings" file:

```
var insertIcon = 'https://sites.google.com/site/scriptsexamples/
    InsertRecordIcon.png';
```

and add an Insert button after the other buttons in the "Record View" file:

```
var insertRecordButton = app.createImage(insertIcon)
    .setVisible(newRecord)
    .setSize('25px', '25px')
    .setId('insertRecordButton')
    .addClickHandler(app.createServerClickHandler('saveRecord')
                  .addCallbackElement(viewRecordTable));
app.getElementById('navPanel').setWidget(0,4, insertRecordButton);
```

This will give a different look to inserting over saving.

Moving over to the "Save Record" file, add an `if` statement to detect the `insertRecord` `Button` press. The `insertFusionObj` method returns the `rowid` for the inserted row, and calling it within the `setValue` method will set the value into the UI all at the same time. It looks a bit tricky but is an easy way to combine functions. Wrap up the `writeFusionObj` call in an `else` statement to keep the Save button working:

```
if(e.parameter.source == 'insertRecordButton'){
  app.getElementById('rowid')
    .setValue(FusionTablesApp.insertFusionObj(e.parameter).toString())
    .setEnabled(false);

}else{
  FusionTablesApp.writeFusionObj(e.parameter);
}
```

After the "Insert" button has been pressed, the user will be returned to "View Only" mode. This means the Insert button needs to be hidden before returning the app:

```
app.getElementById('insertRecordButton').setVisible(false);
```

Reload the UI page and create a record. After inserting the record, do a search and you will see the new record in the search results.

Deleting a Record

At this point you could probably guess how to delete a record, but we will go through the steps one last time so your application is polished and ready to deploy.

Back in the "Settings" file, add a "Delete" icon:

```
var deleteIcon = 'https://sites.google.com/site/scriptsexamples/killRecord.png';
```

In the "Record View" file, add the "Delete" button after the others, and set the handler to execute the deleteRecord function:

```
var deleteButton = app.createImage(deleteIcon)
    .setVisible(false)
    .setSize('25px', '25px')
    .setId('deleteButton')
    .addClickHandler(app.createServerClickHandler('deleteRecord')
                    .addCallbackElement(viewRecordTable));
app.getElementById('navPanel').setWidget(0,5, deleteButton);
```

After saving a file, the "Delete" icon needs to be switched off; that happens at the end of the "Save Record" file:

```
app.getElementById('deleteButton').setVisible(false);
```

UI details out of the way, create a new "Delete Record" file and add a delete call to the Fusion Table. The UI will need to be updated with a message that the removal has taken place and the buttons reset to the beginning state:

```
function deleteRecord(e){
  var app = UiApp.getActiveApplication();

  FusionTablesApp.deleteFusionRow(e.parameter.rowid);

  app.getElementById('contentGrid')
     .setWidget(0,0, app.createLabel('Record has been Deleted forever!'));

  app.getElementById('cancelButton').setVisible(false);
  app.getElementById('saveButton').setVisible(false);
  app.getElementById('newFileButton').setVisible(true);
  app.getElementById('deleteButton').setVisible(false);

  return app;
}
```

application is done; take a deep breath. As a final test, reload the UI page and create ew record. Do a search for the record and press the Edit button. Add some more ormation and click Save. Edit again and click Delete.

Where you go from here is a matter of customizing the core functionality you have built in this chapter.

Full Code

You can find all of the code for the files below on this book's Google Drive (*http://bit.ly/ch7-code*).

Code for *settings.gs*.

```
var statusValues = ['Open', 'Pending', 'Closed'];

var logoImage = 'https://sites.google.com/site/scriptsexamples/
scriptGear.png';
var startImage = 'https://sites.google.com/site/scriptsexamples/
RecordsKeeper.png';

//button icons
var searchIcon = 'https://sites.google.com/site/scriptsexamples/
searchicon.png';
var newFileIcon = 'https://sites.google.com/site/scriptsexamples/
newFileIcon.png';
var editIcon = 'https://sites.google.com/site/scriptsexamples/editIcon.png';
var cancelIcon = 'https://sites.google.com/site/scriptsexamples/CancelIcon.png';
var saveIcon = 'https://sites.google.com/site/scriptsexamples/saveicon.png';
var insertIcon = 'https://sites.google.com/site/scriptsexamples/InsertRecordI-
con.png';
var deleteIcon = 'https://sites.google.com/site/scriptsexamples/killRecord.png';

function setup(){
FusionTableApp.setFusionId('1RCEec2uDQXprJTDKurRuR55Xsn2kS4wYJnS4kec');
FusionTableApp.setClientId('434188666232.apps.googleusercontent.com');
FusionTableApp.setClientSecret('IBQwebGJf9xueDJmNzQbgTBg');
Logger.log(FusionTableApp.getFusionHeaders());
}
```

Code for *CSS.gs*.

```
function applyCSS_(element, style){
  for (var key in style){
    element.setStyleAttribute(key, style[key]);
  }
}

  var _headerGrid =
      {
      "border-bottom":"2px solid #404040"
      }
```

```
    var _rows =
       {
       "border-bottom":"2px solid #C0C0C0     "
       }
```

Code for *doGet.gs.*

```
function doGet(e) {
    var app = UiApp.createApplication().setTitle('Record Manager');

    var mainPanel = app.createVerticalPanel();
    app.add(mainPanel);

    var headerGrid = app.createGrid(1,3).setId('headerGrid').setWidth('500px');
    mainPanel.add(headerGrid);
    applyCSS_(headerGrid, _headerGrid);

    var logo = app.createImage(logoImage).setSize('30px', '30px');
    headerGrid.setWidget(0,0,logo);
    headerGrid.setWidget(0,1, loadSearchBox(app)); //search component
    headerGrid.setWidget(0,2,loadNavigation(app)); //navigation component

    var contentGrid = app.createGrid(1,1).setId('contentGrid').setWidth('100%');
    mainPanel.add(contentGrid);

    var splash = app.createImage(startImage).setSize('500px', '500px');
    contentGrid.setWidget(0,0, splash);

    return app;
}
```

Code for *Search Component.gs.*

```
function loadSearchBox(app) {

    var app = UiApp.getActiveApplication();
    var searchGrid = app.createGrid(1,3).setId('searchGrid');

    var searchBox = app.createTextBox();
        searchBox.setName('searchBox')
          .setId('searchBox')
          .addKeyUpHandler(app.createServerHandler('searchView')
          .addCallbackElement(searchBox));
    searchGrid.setWidget(0,0, searchBox);

    var searchButton = app.createImage(searchIcon)
        .setSize('25px', '25px')
        .setId('searchButton')
        .addClickHandler(app.createServerHandler('searchView')
        .addCallbackElement(searchBox));
    searchGrid.setWidget(0,1, searchButton);
```

```
      return searchGrid;
  }
```

Code for *Navigation Component.gs*.

```
function loadNavigation(app) {
  var navPanel = app.createGrid(1,6).setId('navPanel');
  var newFileButton = app.createImage(newFileIcon)
      .setSize('25px', '25px')
      .setId('newFileButton')
      .addClickHandler(app.createServerClickHandler('viewRecord'));
  navPanel.setWidget(0,0, newFileButton);
  return navPanel;
}
```

Code for *Search View.gs*.

```
function searchView(e){
  var app = UiApp.getActiveApplication();
  if (e.parameter.source=='searchBox' && e.parameter.keyCode!=13 ||
                               e.parameter.searchBox=='') {

    return app;
  }

  var searchPanel = app.createVerticalPanel();
  app.getElementById('contentGrid').setWidget(0,0, searchPanel);
  var searchHeader = app.createFlexTable().setCellPadding(5);
  searchPanel.add(searchHeader);
  applyCSS_(searchHeader, _headerGrid);

  var searchTable = app.createFlexTable().setId('searchTable');
  searchPanel.add(searchTable);

  var searchKey = e.parameter.searchBox;
  var arrayResult1 = FusionTableApp.searchFusion("'First Name', 'Last Name'",
    "'First Name'"+" CONTAINS IGNORING CASE '"+ searchKey+"'");
  var arrayResult2 = FusionTableApp.searchFusion("'First Name', 'Last Name'",
    "'Last Name'"+" CONTAINS IGNORING CASE '"+ searchKey+"'");

  arrayResult2.splice(0,1);
  var concatArray = arrayResult1.concat(arrayResult2);
  var fusionSearch = ObjApp.rangeToObjects(concatArray);
  for (i in concatArray[0]){
    if (concatArray[0][i]=='rowid')
      continue;
    searchHeader.setWidget(0, parseInt(i), app.createLabel(concatArray[0][i])
                                  .setWidth('150px'));
  }

  for(j in fusionSearch){
    var record = app.createFlexTable().setId(fusionSearch[j].rowid)
        .setCellPadding(5)
        .addClickHandler(app.createServerClickHandler('viewRecord'));
    applyCSS_(record, _rows);
```

```
      for (i in concatArray[0]){
        if (arrayResult1[0][i]=='rowid')
          continue;

      record.setWidget(parseInt(j), parseInt(i),
              app.createLabel(fusionSearch[j][ObjApp
                  .camelString(concatArray[0][i])])
                  .setWidth('150px')
                  .addMouseOverHandler(app.createClientHandler()
                  .forTargets(app.getElementById(fusionSearch[j].rowid))
                  .setStyleAttribute('color', 'blue')
                  .setStyleAttribute('background', 'FFFF99'))
                  .addMouseOutHandler(app.createClientHandler()
                  .forTargets(app.getElementById(fusionSearch[j].rowid))
                  .setStyleAttribute('color', 'black')
                  .setStyleAttribute('background', 'transparent'))
              );
      }

    searchTable.setWidget(parseInt(j), 0, record);
    }

    return app;
  }
```

Code for *Record View.gs.*

```
  function viewRecord(e) {
    var app = UiApp.getActiveApplication();
    var newRecord = false;

    if (e.parameter.source == 'cancelButton'){
      var recordId = e.parameter.rowid;
      app.getElementById('newFileButton').setVisible(true);
    }else{
      var recordId = e.parameter.source;
    }

    if (e.parameter.source == 'newFileButton'){
      var arrayheaders = FusionTableApp.getFusionHeaders();
      arrayheaders.push('rowid');
      var arrayResult = [arrayheaders]
      var fusionRecord = new Object();
      newRecord = true;
    }else{


      var arrayResult = FusionTableApp.searchFusion("*", "'rowid' = '"+
      recordId+"'");
      var fusionRecord = ObjApp.rangeToObjects(arrayResult)[0];
    }
```

```
var viewRecordTable = app.createFlexTable().setCellPadding(5)
.setId('viewRecordTable');
app.getElementById('contentGrid').setWidget(0,0, viewRecordTable);

for (var i in arrayResult[0]){
  switch (arrayResult[0][i]){

    case 'Status':
      viewRecordTable.setWidget(parseInt(i), 0,
      app.createLabel(arrayResult[0][i]));
      var status = app.createListBox()
                    .setId(ObjApp.camelString(arrayResult[0][i]))
                    .setName(ObjApp.camelString(arrayResult[0][i]))
                    .addItem(fusionRecord[ObjApp
                    .camelString(arrayResult[0][i])])
                    .setWidth('100px').setEnabled(newRecord);
      viewRecordTable.setWidget(parseInt(i), 1, status);

      for (k in statusValues){
        if (statusValues[k] != fusionRecord[ObjApp
        .camelString(arrayResult[0][i])])
        status.addItem(statusValues[k]);
      }
      break;

    case 'Notes':
      viewRecordTable.setWidget(parseInt(i), 0,
      app.createLabel(arrayResult[0][i]));
      viewRecordTable.setWidget(parseInt(i), 1, app
          .createTextArea()
          .setSize('350px', '100px')
          .setId(ObjApp.camelString(arrayResult[0][i]))
          .setName(ObjApp.camelString(arrayResult[0][i]))
          .setValue(fusionRecord[ObjApp.camelString(arrayResult[0][i])])
          .setEnabled(newRecord)
      );
      break;

    case 'rowid':
      //no label required but the values need to be passed in e.parameter
      viewRecordTable.setWidget(parseInt(i), 1, app.createTextBox()
          .setId(ObjApp.camelString(arrayResult[0][i]))
          .setName(ObjApp.camelString(arrayResult[0][i]))
          .setValue(fusionRecord[ObjApp.camelString(arrayResult[0][i])])
          .setVisible(false) //hide the row
      );
      break;

    default:
      viewRecordTable.setWidget(parseInt(i), 0,
          app.createLabel(arrayResult[0][i]));
      viewRecordTable.setWidget(parseInt(i), 1, app.createTextBox()
```

```
                              .setId(ObjApp.camelString(arrayResult[0][i]))
                              .setName(ObjApp.camelString(arrayResult[0][i]))
                              .setValue(fusionRecord[ObjApp
                              .camelString(arrayResult[0][i])])
                              .setWidth('350px').setEnabled(newRecord)
                          );
        break;
    }
}

var editButton = app.createImage(editIcon)
    .setVisible(true)
    .setSize('25px', '25px')
    .setId('editButton')
    .addClickHandler(app.createServerClickHandler('editRecord')
                    .addCallbackElement(viewRecordTable));
app.getElementById('navPanel').setWidget(0, 1, editButton);

var cancelButton = app.createImage(cancelIcon)
    .setVisible(false)
    .setSize('25px', '25px')
    .setId('cancelButton')
    .addClickHandler(app.createServerClickHandler('viewRecord')
                    .addCallbackElement(viewRecordTable));
app.getElementById('navPanel').setWidget(0, 3, cancelButton);

var saveButton = app.createImage(saveIcon)
    .setVisible(false)
    .setSize('25px', '25px')
    .setId('saveButton')
    .addClickHandler(app.createServerClickHandler('saveRecord')
                    .addCallbackElement(viewRecordTable));
app.getElementById('navPanel').setWidget(0,2, saveButton);

var insertRecordButton = app.createImage(insertIcon)
    .setVisible(newRecord)
    .setSize('25px', '25px')
    .setId('insertRecordButton')
    .addClickHandler(app.createServerClickHandler('saveRecord')
                    .addCallbackElement(viewRecordTable));
app.getElementById('navPanel').setWidget(0,4, insertRecordButton);

var deleteButton = app.createImage(deleteIcon)
    .setVisible(false)
    .setSize('25px', '25px')
    .setId('deleteButton')
    .addClickHandler(app.createServerClickHandler('deleteRecord')
                    .addCallbackElement(viewRecordTable));
app.getElementById('navPanel').setWidget(0,5, deleteButton);


if(newRecord)
```

```
        editButton.setVisible(false);

    return app;
  }
```

Code for *Edit Record.gs.*

```
    function editRecord(e){
      var app = UiApp.getActiveApplication();

      var headers = ObjApp.camelArray(FusionTableApp.getFusionHeaders());

      for (i in headers){
        app.getElementById(headers[i]).setEnabled(true);
      }

      app.getElementById('editButton').setVisible(false);
      app.getElementById('newFileButton').setVisible(false);
      app.getElementById('cancelButton').setVisible(true);
      app.getElementById('saveButton').setVisible(true);
      app.getElementById('deleteButton').setVisible(true);


      return app;
    }
```

Code for *Save Record.gs.*

```
    function saveRecord(e){
      var app = UiApp.getActiveApplication();

      if(e.parameter.source == 'insertRecordButton'){
        app.getElementById('rowid')
          .setValue(FusionTableApp.insertFusionObj(e.parameter)
          .toString())
          .setEnabled(false);

      }else{
        FusionTableApp.writeFusionObj(e.parameter);
      }

      var headers = ObjApp.camelArray(FusionTableApp.getFusionHeaders());

      for (i in headers){
          app.getElementById(headers[i]).setEnabled(false);
      }

      app.getElementById('cancelButton').setVisible(false);
      app.getElementById('saveButton').setVisible(false);
      app.getElementById('newFileButton').setVisible(true);
      app.getElementById('editButton').setVisible(true);
      app.getElementById('insertRecordButton').setVisible(false);
      app.getElementById('deleteButton').setVisible(false);
```

```
      return app;
    }
```

Code for *Delete Record.gs*.

```
function deleteRecord(e){
  var app = UiApp.getActiveApplication();

  FusionTableApp.deleteFusionRow(e.parameter.rowid);

  app.getElementById('contentGrid')
     .setWidget(0,0, app.createLabel('Record has been Deleted forever!'));

  app.getElementById('cancelButton').setVisible(false);
  app.getElementById('saveButton').setVisible(false);
  app.getElementById('newFileButton').setVisible(true);
  app.getElementById('deleteButton').setVisible(false);

  return app;
}
```

CHAPTER 8

Document Workflows

Back in the day, circa 2007, I was working at the New Mexico Attorney General's Office, attempting to streamline the legislative bill analyses we performed each year. It was a crazy time for the office, with more than 1,000 bills going through the office in 30 days, legislators calling to get the latest updates, and politics galore. Honestly, to this day I'm baffled by how it all gets done while keeping the mortality rate so low.

The process starts with a legislator submitting a bill for analysis. The bill is assigned to different attorneys depending on their area of practice, who write an analysis and send it off to reviewers, who may send it to others who make edits and send it back or to someone else, and so on until the final approval, where the analysis is sent back to the legislator. That sounds simple enough, but add a 24-hour deadline and politically charged issues, and it's a recipe for a heart attack. Adding to the mayhem, the team at the legislative building and the upper management never knew what was being analyzed or where in the queue something might be. Not the best position to be in when the chairman is fuming about a delay.

At the time, I thought we could add in a little technology to smooth out the flow of work —and wouldn't you know it, we had just installed SharePoint. It had workflows that we hoped to leverage into an email approval and tracking system. After a few weeks we eked out a rudimentary system that sort of worked most of the time. The system had a painful learning curve and was not very flexible in its capabilities. Once a workflow started, it had to go through until it was done and could not be changed. It only worked in the office and not at all from BlackBerry devices. When we finally rolled it out, several early failures caused the staff to lose interest, and they slipped back to the old way of doing things. Epic project failure.

The good news is that times have changed, and so have the tools available to handle workflows.

Building a Modern Email Workflow

Google Docs and Gmail are powerful tools for creation and collaboration, but they don't do workflow in the sense of a series of tasks being tracked and completed by different people. This is a gap that Google Apps Script can bridge.

These days people are busy and on the go; they can't be expected to hang out at their desks all day waiting for something to arrive for signing. Google Docs works on everything, virtually anywhere, and that is what makes it such a powerful tool. Why shouldn't your workflow system be integrated and take advantage of the be-anywhere cloud platform that Google Apps runs on?

In this chapter, you will create a document workflow builder that has a flexible nature, which will fit many situations and can be customized on the fly by the users without any coding on their part. It will take advantage of Google Docs for file management, Gmail for notifications, and Google Apps Script to give users an interface right in the document sidebar. The application is robust, meaning workflows can be restarted or redirected, approvers can be added during runtime, there can be parallel approvers, and you can add other great workflow features.

What You Will Learn

You will learn about:

- Building a sidebar app
- ScriptDB
- Gmail integration
- Accessing Google Documents
- Deploying as an add-on

Supplies

You will need:

- A Google account
- A good grasp of the concepts and terminology used in Part I

Application Overview

The application will be launched from a custom menu in your Google Doc; then the owner can add approvers or view other information about the workflow. When the workflow is started, an email is sent to the approvers asking them to come and look at the document. They will also see the Approvals menu and be able to approve the document (Figure 8-1).

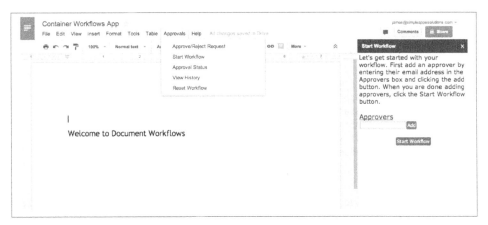

Figure 8-1. Simple yet powerful, a good workflow can smooth out the bumps of the workday

As part of the workflow, you will have the option to review the entire history, including approval status changes and approvers who have been added to or removed from the workflow. This acts as an audit log and will stay with the document for future reference.

Creating the Menus

Our app is going to run from a custom menu item in a Google Doc. Recall that this kind of app is called a *container app* because the code itself is held in a document or spreadsheet and runs as part of that container.

First, we'll create a new document and script from the Tools menu. We'll break this app into several sections: each choice in the menu will have its own HTML file (this makes it easier to follow what's going on in the development). Here are the files we will be creating:

- *Code.gs*
- *ApproveRejectRequest.html*
- *StartWorkflow.html*
- *ApprovalStatus.html*
- *ViewHistory.html*

- *ResetWorkflow.html*
- *Styles.html*

We start our journey in the *Code.gs* file by adding the menus:

```
var ui = DocumentApp.getUi();

function onOpen() {
    ui
        .createMenu('Approvals')
        .addItem('Approve/Reject Request', 'approveRejectRequest')
        .addItem('Start Workflow', 'startWorkflow')
        .addItem('Approval Status', 'approvalStatus')
        .addItem('View History', 'viewHistory')
        .addItem('Reset Workflow', 'resetWorkflow')
        .addToUi();
}
```

To add things to the document's menu and the window itself, we call `DocumentApp.ge tUi()`, which is similar to the jQuery `$` function but limits what we can access.

In this section we will be calling on the `DocumentApp` over and over, so we will save it as a global variable outside any function but available to all.

We want the menu to appear for use when the document is opened, so we will use the special `onOpen` function in Google Apps Script to do our work.

onOpen is one of those special built-in triggers that Google Apps Script uses to run automatically.

Others include:

- onEdit
- onInstall
- onFormSubmit
- doGet
- doPost

Make sure you don't use these as your function names, or you may get some unexpected behavior.

You create a menu with `createMenu(<Your Menu Title>)` and then add submenu items using `addItem(<Submenu Title>, <Function to Run>)`. There is also an `.addSepa rator` method that helps you organize the menu.

Once you're done adding all the submenu items, you use `.addToUi;` to actually insert the menu. At this time there is no way to control the order of menus in the Doc, so yours will always go to the left of "Help" (see Figure 8-2). One other thing to note is that you can add several menus to the menu bar.

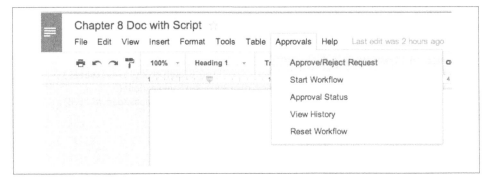

Figure 8-2. Approvals menu installed

Right now, clicking on one of the submenu items doesn't do anything. In the next section we will be adding functions to handle each menu request and adding the files that correspond to the operations.

Loading the Sidebar

Workflows come in many flavors: some are entirely done through email, others send email notices and have a web interface, and still others are application-specific and do not communicate outside at all. The Workflow application in this chapter takes the middle road: a UI in the document for building and managing the workflow, and a notification system to send emails. The two systems are tightly integrated, but notifications will be bolted on after we get the manager section completed.

In the last section you created the menus and added some functions to run when a particular submenu was clicked. Still working in the *Code.gs* file, add in the following functions:

```
function startWorkflow() {
var html = HtmlService.createTemplateFromFile('startWorkflow').evaluate()
    .setTitle('Start Workflow').setWidth(300).setSandboxMode(
                                HtmlService.SandboxMode.NATIVE);
  ui.showSidebar(html);
}

function approveRejectRequest() {
var html = HtmlService.createTemplateFromFile('ApproveRejectRequest').evaluate()
    .setTitle('Approve/Reject Request').setWidth(300).setSandboxMode(
                                HtmlService.SandboxMode.NATIVE);
```

```
    ui.showSidebar(html);
}

function approvalStatus() {
var html = HtmlService.createTemplateFromFile('ApprovalStatus').evaluate()
    .setTitle('Approval Status').setWidth(300).setSandboxMode(
                                HtmlService.SandboxMode.NATIVE);
  ui.showSidebar(html);
}

function viewHistory() {
var html = HtmlService.createTemplateFromFile('ViewHistory').evaluate()
    .setTitle('View History').setWidth(300).setSandboxMode(
                                HtmlService.SandboxMode.NATIVE);
  ui.showSidebar(html);
}

function resetWorkflow() {
var html = HtmlService.createTemplateFromFile('ResetWorkflow').evaluate()
    .setTitle('Reset Workflow').setWidth(300).setSandboxMode(
                                HtmlService.SandboxMode.NATIVE);
  ui.showSidebar(html);
}
```

By now you should know that this is the HtmlService, which returns HTML. The good
news is that container app UIs can also be built using HTML. In each of these functions
we are using HtmlService to get a file (which you will create from the list of files in the
previous section). To open the sidebar and show the HTML content, we use ui.show
Sidebar(html). When you're done creating files and adding your code, your editor
should look much like Figure 8-3.

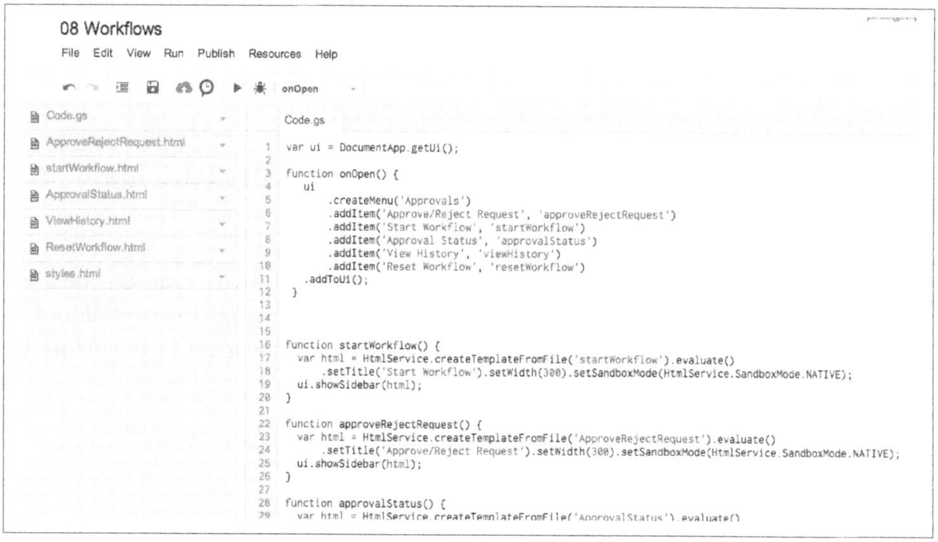

Figure 8-3. Files have been created and functions are ready

Starting the Workflow

Now that you have the menu in place, along with functions to load the correct sidebars and HTML files, it's time to create the first UI. What better place to start than with the Start Workflow operation?

Open the *startWorkflow.html* file, and let's dig in.

Start Workflow HTML

On this page we want to be able to tell the user what the application does, give a method for adding and removing approvers as well as list them, and provide a button to start the workflow process:

```
<div id="wrapper">
  <div>
    <span>Let's get started with your workflow. First add an approver
        by entering
    their email address in the Approvers box and clicking the add button.
    When you are done adding approvers, click the Start Workflow button.</span>
  </div>
  <br>
  <div>
    <span class="sectionHeader">Approvers</span><br>
    <div id="approvers"></div>
    <div>
      <form id="addApprover">
        <input type="email" id="approver" placeholder="Email Address">
```

```
      <input type="submit" class="button blueButton" value="Add">
    </form>
  </div>
</div>
<br>
<div class="center">
  <span id="startButton" class="button redButton">Start Workflow</span>
</div>
</div>
```

When you're building an app like this, which will have several different user displays, it's a good idea to wrap each "page" in a div so that you can change the overall look by simply changing the CSS file. In this case we use `<div id="wrapper">` to enclose the HTML section, much as you might use a body tag.

Here is the CSS for the wrapper div, which should go in the *styles.html* file:

```
#wrapper {
  margin:2px 4px 3px 4px;
  font-family: Verdana, Geneva, sans-serif;
}
```

The next div is where you put the instructions. For this app there is no specific style for this section, but you could easily add some CSS tags to get the effect you want.

Now we dig into the dynamic sections, which are going to require tags both for formatting and to add information using jQuery. First is the Approvers section. Because there will be other sections in the different parts of our app that also use section headers, we will style them all the same using `class="sectionHeader"` and its CSS:

```
.sectionHeader {
  color: #202020 ;
  font-size: 18px;
  text-decoration:underline;
  margin-bottom: 20px;
}
```

We add `<div id="approvers"></div>` as a place to load the list of approvers that we are going to retrieve from our database.

Directly after the approvers header is the form that will allow the user to add approvers:

```
<form id="addApprover">
  <input type="email" id="approver" placeholder="Email Address">
  <input type="submit" class="button blueButton" value="Add">
</form>
```

We use formal form format here, so we can take advantage of the HTML5 email validation. We want more of a Google-y look for our buttons, so we round the corners and such in the CSS. Different buttons will need to be different colors, so we take advantage of the cascading effect in CSS to make modifications. Lastly, the button should do something to let the user know it's interactive; we do that with the hover opacity effect:

```
.button {
  color: #FFFFFF;
  font-size: 12px;
  moz-border-radius: 3px;
  -webkit-border-radius: 3px;
  padding: 3px;
}

.addApprover {
  background-color: #3366FF;
}

.redButton {
  background-color: #C80000;
}

.button:hover{
  opacity:0.7;
}

.center {
  text-align: center;
}
```

The form will be accessed through its id ("addApprover") when we add event handlers. The last part of the HTML section is the Start button, which we use the span tag for:

```
<span id="startButton" class="button redButton">Start Workflow</span>
```

It gets the button and redButton CSS classes to make it look just right. That ends the HTML section of the Start Workflow operation, but in order to make all that CSS work you will need to import the *styles.html* sheet:

```
<?!= HtmlService.createHtmlOutputFromFile('styles').getContent(); ?>
```

You can now run Start Workflow from the Approvals menu (Figure 8-4).

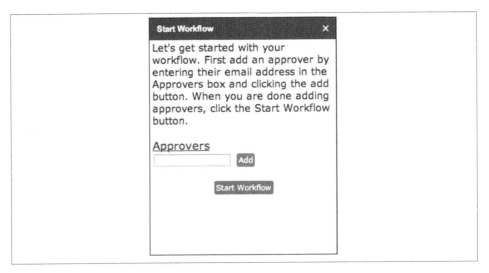

Figure 8-4. The Start Workflow UI

Start Workflow JavaScript

Now that the UI looks right, we can get started with making it do something. jQuery is a great way to simplify working in web pages, so let's add that now:

```
<script src="http://ajax.googleapis.com/ajax/libs/jquery/1.8.3/jquery.min.js">
</script>
```

It's always a good idea to wait until everything is loaded on the page before running our JavaScript, so we use the `ready` method and grab all the HTML by calling the docu ment element:

```
<script>
     $(document).ready(function() {
        //bind click handlers at runtime
        $('#addApprover').submit(addApprover);
        $('#startButton').click(startWorkflow);
        getApprovers();

     });
</script>
```

When we created the HTML earlier, we gave the "Form" and "Start" buttons unique IDs that we can now access and assign event handlers to. `addApprover` is the form, and because we want to handle both the "Enter" key and someone clicking on the "Add" button, we use the `submit` method to run the function `addApprover`, which we will create in a few minutes. We'll create `getApprovers` after that.

Similarly, we get the `startButton`, and because it will only be clicked we use the `click` event, which will fire the function `startWorkflow`.

The first thing the user will want to do here is to add an approver, so that's where we start:

```
function addApprover(){
  google.script.run.withSuccessHandler(function() {
    getApprovers();
    $('#approver').val('');
  }).addApprover($("#approver").val());
}
```

Using ScriptDB

We are going to be using Google Apps Script's *ScriptDB* to store our data, so we can retrieve it any time the app runs. For this style of application this is a great option and very easy to use. ScriptDB is a JavaScript object database that uses a *JSON* (JavaScript Object Notation) type architecture to store and serve data.

 ScriptDB is a perfect solution for small data stores, but it can only go up to 50 MB per developer. In a nutshell, you have 50 MB for all your projects. If you think your application will be extremely popular, I would recommend using Google's Cloud SQL for your storage needs.

Because ScriptDB is a server-side service, we will need to send our approver to a backend process that uses the google.script.run method and a server function we will create called addApprover. That's interesting—two functions with the same name? We can get away with this because the JavaScript in the HTML page is in a different *scope*. This is personal preference: some like things to line up, where others might want to use something like addApproverClient and addApproverServer.

The text box IDed as #approver holds the email address, and we get it and send it to the server like this:

```
google.script.run.withSuccessHandler(function() {
      }).addApprover($("#approver").val());
```

We don't need anything back from the server when it returns, but we do need to do some things on the client side. One is to clear the email box, and the other is to update the list of approvers.

Add into the server call function:

```
getApprovers();
$('#approver').val('');
```

Adding Approvers

Switch over to the *Code.gs* file and create an `addApprover` function. The whole function looks like this; so you won't get lost, we'll break it apart next:

```
function addApprover(email){
  var db = ScriptDb.getMyDb();
  var docId = DocumentApp.getActiveDocument().getId();
  var ob =    {
                docId: docId,
                approverEmail: email,
                status: null,
                emailSent: false
              }
  db.save(ob);

  var history = {
                docId: docId,
                action: 'Added Approver',
                email: email,
                date: Utilities.formatDate(new Date(), "GMT", "MM-dd-yyyy'
'HH:mm:ss")
              }
  db.save(history);
}
```

The function takes one argument, `email`, which we sent from the form. Every Google Apps Script comes with a ScriptDB all ready to go called `MyDb`. This is accessed by calling `ScriptDb.getMyDb`, which we store in a variable called `db`—cryptic, I know. Anyway, what we need to do next is to build a JSON object and insert it into our database (DB). Your DB might contain information from several docs, so to keep everything sorted out you need to get this document's ID using:

```
DocumentApp.getActiveDocument().getId();
```

Now that we have all the information, the object is built like this:

```
var ob =    {
              docId: docId,
              approverEmail: email,
              status: null,
              emailSent: false
            }
```

You know about the `docId` and `approverEmail`, but what are the other values? One thing we want to allow users to do is give their approval, but what if they reject the document? The `status` property is where we will store this information.

When you start the workflow, all the approvers you've added need to get an email asking them to come and approve or reject your document. If you add more approvers later, you don't want to resend the email to those approvers who already got the first email.

This property will keep that from happening. Don't worry: we will add a Send Reminder button in the Approval Status operation to gently nudge those deadbeats who haven't given their two cents.

To save your ob to the DB you use:

```
db.save(ob);
```

Having an audit log of everything that happened in the approval process keeps everything on the up and up, just in case there is a dispute later. It's simply another entry in the DB, which we call history.

Because it needs to know what happened, we set action and date properties:

```
action: 'Added Approver',
...
date: Utilities.formatDate(new Date(), "GMT", "MM-dd-yyyy' 'HH:mm:ss")
```

That wraps up the addApprover server-side process, and we can now head back to where we returned back to the addApprover client-side function in the *startWorkflow.html* file.

Loading the Approvers

You have seen getApprovers a few times now—and I'm sorry that I keep putting it off —but before you start retrieving information from the DB, I wanted you to see how it got there in the first place. Now that you have a method for saving to the DB, let's go get that information.

Add the following function inside the closing script tag in the *startWorkflow.html* file:

```
function getApprovers(){
    google.script.run.withSuccessHandler(function(approvers) {
      $("#approvers").html('');
      for(var i =0; i < approvers.length; i++){
        $("#approvers").append(
          '<img class="approver" email="'+approvers[i].approverEmail+'"
          title="Click to remove this Approver"'+
            'src="https://googledrive.com/host/0B61-C9Nl4dO-ZEpvTk9SWU5tYnc/
x_ico1.png"
          width="12px"><span> '+approvers[i].approverEmail+'</span><br>'
        );
      }
      $('.approver').on('click', function() {
        removeApprover($(this).attr('email'));
      });
    }).getApprovers();
```

Right off you see we are calling to the server, and if you go down to the end, you see we have asked for the getApprovers server-side function. Yes, it has an "s" on the end, meaning it's a different function than what you just finished creating.

I don't want to trip you up here, but we really do need to head back over to the *Code.gs* file to understand what we are going to send into the return of the server call. I will keep calling out which file we are in so you don't get lost.

Switch back to *Code.gs* and add this function:

```
function getApprovers(){
  var docId = DocumentApp.getActiveDocument().getId();
  var db = ScriptDb.getMyDb();
  var result = db.query({docId: docId, approverEmail: db.anyValue()});
  var approvers =[];
  while (result.hasNext()) {
    approvers.push(result.next());
  }
  return approvers;
}
```

We are going to load up the DB and then run a query for all the entries that match the docId and have a value in approverEmail. Then we use a while statement to iterate the result and add all the entries to the approvers array, which will look like this:

```
[{approverEmail=James@apps4gapps.com,  status=null,  docId=1ldLP-sewoT8,  email-
Sent=false}]
```

That wasn't a long detour: now we can return with this function to the *startWork-flow.html* file.

The getApprovers function needs to run when the page is loaded and after adding an approver to the list. The approver list is written to the approvers div, and we will be using the jQuery method append. Before we start adding, though, we need to clear that element, so there are never duplicate entries:

```
$("#approvers").html('');
```

When the server returns, we save the value in the approvers argument, and we can now iterate through that array.

Here is what each line will look like:

```
'<img class="approver" email="'+approvers[i].approverEmail+'"  title="Click to
remove this
Approver"'+'src="https://googledrive.com/host/0B61-C9Nl4dO-ZEpvTk9SWU5tYnc/
x_ico1.png"
width="12px"><span> '+approvers[i].approverEmail+'</span><br>'
```

We get an image that I've saved for you in Drive: an *X*, the universal sign used to remove an approver. Then we access the approvers array and the approverEmail to finish the listing.

You will need to add a click handler to the *X* image to make it actually do something:

```
$('.approver').on('click', function() {
    removeApprover($(this).attr('email'));
});
```

Did you notice another function firing there? There will be yet another client/server interaction coming up, but first save all your work and run the Start Workflow menu item. After the UI loads in the sidebar, add a few emails to the list to test it out. Figure 8-5 shows where you are at this point.

Figure 8-5. Start Workflow is now saving approvers

Removing Approvers

"Rinse and Repeat" would be a good title for the next few sections, as we will continue to attach events to buttons and then fire off data to the server and process what we get back.

Remember that *X* from the last section where we added a click handler? That function was for `removeApprover`, and we sent the email address in the arguments. Here is the code for the `removeApprover` function, which does not return anything—but it does reload the approvers `div`, so the user can see that there was indeed a change in the list.

Add the following code to the *startWorkflow.html* file:

```
function removeApprover(approver){ //client side
    google.script.run.withSuccessHandler(function() {
        getApprovers();
    }).removeApprover(approver);
}
```

On the server side we have another `removeApprover` function, which will query the DB and completely remove that entry. Wait a minute, though: we said there needs to be an audit trail of everything that goes on with our approval system. While we are removing from the approvers, we need to add more information about that change to the `histo ry`. The entry for removing an approver is almost exactly the same as that for adding one to the `history`, with the exception of the `action` property, which we set to Removed Approver.

Here is the addition to the *Code.gs* file:

```
function removeApprover(email){ //server side
  var docId = DocumentApp.getActiveDocument().getId();
  var db = ScriptDb.getMyDb();
  var result = db.query({docId: docId, approverEmail: email});
  db.remove(result.next());

  var history =  {
          docId: docId,
          action: 'Removed Approver',
          email: email,
            date: Utilities.formatDate(new Date(), "GMT", "MM-dd-yyyy'
'HH:mm:ss")
        }
  db.save(history);
}
```

Pressing Start

At last it's time to get this workflow started. We attached a click handler to the "Start" button much earlier in the chapter. Here is the function it runs, which you should add to *startWorkflow.html*:

```
function startWorkflow(){ //client side
  google.script.run.withSuccessHandler(function() {
    $('#wrapper').html('OK, I have sent emails to the approvers. <br>
    You can see their responses from the Approval Status menu.')
  }).start();
}
```

Not only does it not take any arguments, but it doesn't return anything either. On the client side, all it really needs to do is update the UI to let the user know that the workflow was started. We do this by replacing all the content in the `wrapper` with a short message.

Back over in the *Code.gs* file, the seemingly simple function on the client side does a bunch of processing on the server:

```
function start(){
  var docId = DocumentApp.getActiveDocument().getId();
  var db = ScriptDb.getMyDb();
  var result = db.query({docId: docId, approverEmail: db.anyValue()});
```

```
while (result.hasNext()) {
  var record = result.next();
  if(record.status == null){
    var doc = DocumentApp.getActiveDocument();
    doc.addEditor(record.approverEmail);
    var url = doc.getUrl();

    MailApp.sendEmail({
        to: record.approverEmail,
        subject: "Please Review my Document",
        htmlBody: 'You have been asked to review and approve a document
        <br>'+
          'Please <a href="'+url+'">Click here</a> to Open the document. '+
          '<br><br>After reviewing click the Approvals menu and select '+
          'Approve/Reject Request',
    });

    record.status = 'Email Sent'
    db.save(record);
  }
 }
}
```

We start by grabbing all the approvers from the DB using the query `approverEmail:`
`db.anyValue()`. Now we can iterate through the results. One thing we don't want to do
is resend emails about approving the workflow to people who have already been notified.
We do this by checking the `status` property for a value. If we do need to send an email,
that person will need access to the document, which we accomplish using the `addEdi`
`tor` method from the DocumentApp Service.

The approver has been granted access, and now all we need to do is send an email using
Google Apps Script's MailApp. One of the great features of MailApp is that it lets you
send HTML body text. To dress up our message, we can add an anchor tag to hide the
long document URL.

We have one more thing to do: again, we don't want multiple emails going to the same
approver, so we now set the `status` property to `Email Sent`.

Let's give it a run and see how it works. Save all your work and reload the app by selecting
Start Workflow from the menu. Make sure you use a valid email address for an account
you can access—the one you are using to build the app will work just fine. Now hit the
Start Workflow button and then check your email. In a few minutes you should receive
the message requesting your approval (Figure 8-6).

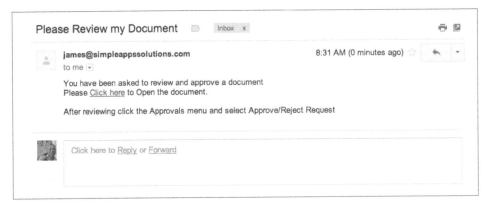

Figure 8-6. Approval message

The messages are sent, and now all we need to do is wait for our approvers to come and… but wait, we haven't given them a way to actually approve the document. In the next section you will be adding a new UI sidebar to give your approvers a way to record their approval status.

Recording Approvals

After receiving your email, the approvers will come and review your document. When they're done, they have been directed to select Approve/Reject Request from the Approvals menu. This will open the sidebar and allow them to select from a list of options about how they would like to respond (Figure 8-7).

Figure 8-7. Approve this document

Jumping right in, we will first work on the HTML in the *ApproveRejectRequest.html* file. Following is the HTML section, which is refreshingly short:

```
<div id="wrapper">
  <div>
    <span>You have been asked to approve this document. Please select your ap-
proval type from the list below. Clicking the Submit button will confirm your
choice and notify the document owner. </span>
  </div>
  <div>
    <br>
    <select id="status">
      <option>Select Approval Type</option>
      <option>Approve &amp; No Edits</option>
      <option>Approve &amp; Allow Edits</option>
      <option>Needs Work</option>
      <option>Delegate</option>
      <option>Doesn't Need My Approval</option>
      <option>Rejected</option>
    </select>
  </div>
    <br>

  <div class="center">
    <span id="submitButton" class="button redButton">Submit</span>
  </div>
</div>
```

Essentially, there is a selection element that provides the drop-down box for the approver to select her choice, and a button to confirm it. You have already done the CSS work, so making this look like the rest of the app is simply a matter of adding the right tags.

Speaking of CSS, we will add it from the *styles.html* file and, while we are at it, also add the jQuery library:

```
<?!= HtmlService.createHtmlOutputFromFile('styles').getContent(); ?>
<script src="http://ajax.googleapis.com/ajax/libs/jquery/1.8.3/jquery.min.js">
</script>
```

Just like in the last section, we use the **ready** method to start adding functionality:

```
<script>
    $(document).ready(function() {
      $('#submitButton').click(submit);

      google.script.run.withSuccessHandler(function(approvers) {
        var notListed = true;
        var user = <?=Session.getEffectiveUser().getEmail()?>;
        for(var i =0; i < approvers.length; i++){
          if(user.toLowerCase() == approvers[i].approverEmail.toLowerCase()){
            notListed = false;
            break;
          }
```

```
        }
        if(notListed){
          $('#wrapper').html('You are not an approver for this Document.')
        }
      }).getApprovers();

    });
  </script>
```

The approver may waffle a bit on her choice and will need to look at what options are available in the drop-down. With this in mind, we don't want to record every time that the approver thinks about this important decision. We therefore attach the click event to the Submit button, requiring that extra step to truly commit.

We don't want just anyone making approvals, and the document may be shared with several people. To take care of this, we will run a check by getting all the approvers using the getApprovers function from *Code.gs*, and then iterating through the list. Google Apps Script has a method called Session.getEffectiveUser().getEmail(), which lets us get the user's email address so we can compare it to the list of approvers in the DB. If the user isn't on the list, we wipe out the whole UI and give her a message. This prevents users from improperly approving documents (Figure 8-8).

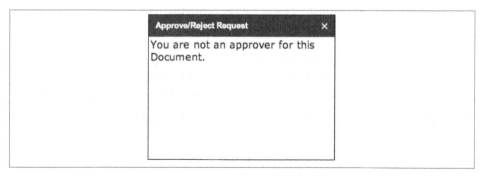

Figure 8-8. You're not approved

If the approver is on the list, we will leave the UI up. After she makes her selection and clicks the Submit button, we need to record the choice. Add the submit function inside the closing script tag:

```
function submit(){
  var email = <?=Session.getEffectiveUser().getEmail()?>;
  var status = $('#status').val();
  google.script.run.withSuccessHandler(function() {
    $('#wrapper').html('Your Approval Status has been recorded.')
  }).setApproverStatus(email, status);
}
```

In this function we will be passing both the approver's email address and her status choice to a new server function called setApproverStatus. After this function returns, we proceed as usual and replace the wrapper HTML content with a message (Figure 8-9).

Figure 8-9. Your Doc has been approved

Move back over to the *Code.gs* file and add the `setApproverStatus` function:

```
function setApproverStatus(email, status){
  var docId = DocumentApp.getActiveDocument().getId();
  var db = ScriptDb.getMyDb();
  var ob = db.query({docId: docId, approverEmail: email}).next();
  if (ob == null)return;
  ob.status = status;
  db.save(ob);

  var history =  {
            docId: docId,
            action: 'Changed Status to: '+status,
            email: email,
              date: Utilities.formatDate(new Date(), "GMT", "MM-dd-yyyy'
'HH:mm:ss")
            }
  db.save(history);
}
```

Here we again open the DB and query for the approver's email, which was sent as an argument from the client function. We then make a change to the `status` property, where we insert the new status, which was also passed as an argument; then we save the DB.

This was a recordable event, so you will also want to reopen the `history` and add another entry about what happened.

At this point you have a working app that lets a user select approvers, automatically share documents, and send emails on how to approve. The app also provides a way for approvers to record their choices. In the next section we are going to have a look at the reporting system that allows us to see the status of the approvers.

Approval Status

The Approval Status dashboard tells us what is going on with this document. We should be able to see who the approvers are and their statuses. One bonus feature is allowing the user to send a reminder to any approver who has not yet responded (Figure 8-10).

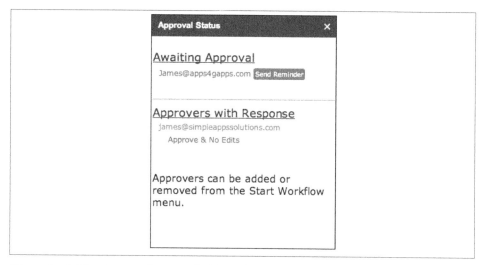

Figure 8-10. The Approval Status dashboard

Open the *ApprovalStatus.html* file. We will start with the HTML:

```html
<div id="wrapper">
  <br>
  <div>
    <span class="sectionHeader">Awaiting Approval</span><br>
    <div class="spaceAfter" id="notApproved"></div>
  </div>
  <br>
  <hr>
  <div>
    <span class="sectionHeader">Approvers with Response</span><br>
    <div id="responded"></div>
  </div>
  <br>
  <br>
  <div>
  Approvers can be added or removed from the Start Workflow menu.
  </div>
</div>
```

Because most of this UI will be dynamically loaded, the HTML is short: it consists of two headers with the sections notApproved and responded under them, waiting for the data.

Now add the CSS and jQuery, then the ready function:

```html
<?!= HtmlService.createHtmlOutputFromFile('styles').getContent(); ?>
<script src="http://ajax.googleapis.com/ajax/libs/jquery/1.8.3/jquery.min.js">
</script>
```

```
<script>
    $(document).ready(function() {
      loadApproverStatus();
    });

</script>
```

Once the window is ready we will run only one function: `loadApproverStatus`. Insert the following inside the closing `script` tag:

```
function loadApproverStatus(){
    google.script.run.withSuccessHandler(function(approvers) {
      for(var i =0; i < approvers.length; i++){
          if(approvers[i].status == null || approvers[i].status =='Email
Sent'){
          $("#notApproved").append('<span class="approverEmail red"> '+
          approvers[i].approverEmail+' </span>'+
          '<span class="reminder" email="'+approvers[i].approverEmail+'">
          Send Reminder</span><br>');
        }else{
          $("#responded").append('<span class="approverEmail green"> '+
          approvers[i].approverEmail+'</span><br>'+
            '<span class="status spaceAfter">'+approvers[i].status+
            '</span><br>');
        }
      }
      $('.reminder').on('click', function() {
              //adds a click handler to each Send Reminder button
          sendReminder($(this).attr('email'));
          $(this).text('Sent');
      });
    }).getApprovers();
  }
```

Breaking this down, we can see that first we call on the server function `getApprovers`, and you know by now that this will return a list of all the approvers.

What else would we do with a list but iterate it and start adding things to placeholders and the divs we reserved? Right off, we need to know if this approver has made a choice, and we do that by checking if his approval status is still set to `null`. If it is, we know he has not approved and can add him to the `notApproved div`. We do this by using append and a `span` tag that holds the approver's email address. Additionally, those who have not responded get a Send Reminder span. Those who have get a status `span`.

Finally, we add a click handler to all the `.reminder` class `divs`, which will run a server-side function called `sendReminder` and after turn the reminder button into the text "Sent."

A `click` event means we have a new function to run. Add the following inside the closing `script` tag:

```
function sendReminder(approver){
  google.script.run.withSuccessHandler(function() {
  }).sendReminder(approver);
}
```

Let's wrap up that server function and then add a bit of style to the divs. Open the *Code.gs* file and add the sendReminder function:

```
function sendReminder(approverEmail){
  MailApp.sendEmail({
          to: approverEmail,
          subject: "Please Review my Document",
          htmlBody: 'You have been asked to review and approve a document
          <br>'+
              'Please <a href="'+DocumentApp.getActiveDocument().getUrl()+'">
              Click here</a> to Open the document.<br><br>'+
              'After reviewing click the Approvals menu and select '+
              'Approve/Reject Request',
  });
}
```

This function takes the approver's email address as the argument and sends an email.

 Because we use the withSuccessHandler feature to make our calls, we don't need to return anything to let the frontend know there was an error. Keep in mind that if an error does occur, the users will not see it, because it is only logged in the console. Instead, they will see that the feature they used does not work.

We want there to be some color emphasis for who has or has not approved, and we also need to make a few other tweaks to these sections to make them more appealing.

Open up the *styles.html* file, and let's add some more CSS:

```
.reminder {
  color: #FFFFFF;
  background-color: #3366FF;
  font-size: 10px;
  moz-border-radius: 3px;
  -webkit-border-radius: 3px;
  padding: 3px;
}

.approverEmail {
  font-size: 12px;
  margin-left: 10px;
  color: #383838;
}

.approverEmail.red {
  color: #C80000;
```

```
}

.approverEmail.green {
  color: #009900;
}

.status {
  color: #686868;
  font-size: 12px;
  margin-left: 25px;
}

.spaceAfter {
  line-height: 25px;
}
```

Reload Approval Status from the menu, and you will get a nicely formatted UI listing of where things stand.

Audit History

At some point someone will ask you about the time an approval was made or dispute ever getting a request for approval. At times like this, you will want to have your ducks in a row and be able to provide an accurate record of everything that went on in your app.

Because there is a menu option for History, we will again use the sidebar and a new UI to display this information. In the *ViewHistory.html* file, get started with the HTML section:

```
<div id="wrapper">
<div>
  <span>These are the actions that have been taken.</span>
</div>
<br>
  <div>
    <div id="approvers"></div>
  </div>
</div>
```

Is it just me, or are these getting shorter? After doing the last section, you can bet this one is much the same: we are reading the DB and loading a div (in this case, approvers with some custom elements).

Now for the script section:

```
<?!= HtmlService.createHtmlOutputFromFile('styles').getContent(); ?>

<script src="http://ajax.googleapis.com/ajax/libs/jquery/1.8.3/jquery.min.js">
</script>
```

```
<script>
    $(document).ready(function() {
      google.script.run.withSuccessHandler(function(history) {
        $("#approvers").html('');
        for(var i =0; i < history.length; i++){
        $("#approvers").append(
          '<span class="sectionHeader">'+history[i].date+'</span><br>'+
          '<span class="approverEmail">'+history[i].email+'</span><br>'+
          '<span class="status">'+history[i].action+'</span><br>'+
          '<hr>'
        );


      }
    }).getHistory();
  });
</script>
```

The history was saved separately from the approvers, so we need a special server function called getHistory to return the items. After that, we will iterate through them to create the look of a chronological history. Different spans are used mainly to make it easy for us to apply the CSS.

Switch to *Code.gs* and add the getHistory function:

```
function getHistory(){
  var docId = DocumentApp.getActiveDocument().getId();
  var db = ScriptDb.getMyDb();
  var result = db.query({docId: docId, action: db.anyValue()});
  var history =[];
  while (result.hasNext()) {
    history.push(result.next());
  }
  var sorted = history.sort(function(a, b) {
  return a.date.replace(/[^0-9.]/g, "") - b.date.replace(/[^0-9.]/g, "")});
  return sorted.reverse();
}
```

After calling on ScriptDB, we query for the action property. This is how we know that the items we get back are history entries rather than approver entries, as approver entries don't have an action property.

 ScriptDB is a JSON store, and there really isn't any order to the items stored in it. This has to do with the object/property relationship in JavaScript. Just because you put things in there in a certain order does not mean they come out that way.

If we returned the history items as they came out of ScriptDB, they might be in any order. While all the events will be listed, the order may be confusing. To solve this, we create a new array and push all the entries into it. Now we can sort that array with a common `a-b` sort function where we compare the data properties. That will get everything in the right order, but from oldest to newest. That might be just the way you like it, but for this example we will use the `reverse` method on the array to go from newest to oldest, so the last thing that happened is right on top. This also looks more like the revision history in Docs, and we like to have things in our apps look similar to the containers they run in.

Save everything and try out the View History selection from the Approvals menu (Figure 8-11).

Figure 8-11. View History

Resetting Everything

Our app does just about everything we set out to accomplish, but what happens if the user made an error and just wants to start over? In this last section we will give users one last UI that lets them get a fresh start.

Open the *ResetWorkflow.html* file and add in this HTML code:

```
<div id="wrapper" class="center">
  <div>
    <span class="warning">Warning!</span><br>
    <span>You are about to reset this workflow. Clicking the Reset button
    will erase all approval history and approvers.</span>
```

```
    </div>
    <br>
    <br>
    <div>
      You can close this window to cancel the reset.<br><br>
      <span id="resetButton" class="button redButton">Confirm Reset</span>
    </div>
  </div>
```

There's not much here but a big warning and a red button, so let's also add the script:

```
<?!= HtmlService.createHtmlOutputFromFile('styles').getContent(); ?>
<script src="http://ajax.googleapis.com/ajax/libs/jquery/1.8.3/jquery.min.js">
</script>

<script>
    $(document).ready(function() {
      $('#resetButton').click(resetWorkflow);
    });

    function resetWorkflow(){
      google.script.run.withSuccessHandler(function() {
        $('#wrapper').html('<h3>The Workflow has been reset</h3>');
      }).reset();
    }
</script>
```

It looks like all we are doing here is firing a server-side function called reset and then presenting a message to the user. We will be going back to the server in just a second, but first open up the *styles.html* file and add this last bit of CSS:

```
.warning {
  color: #C80000;
  font-size: 24px;
}
```

We really, really don't want anyone to miss that, now do we? (See Figure 8-12.)

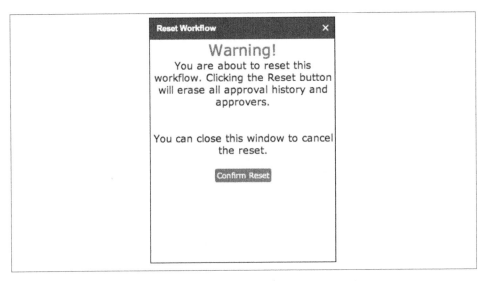

Figure 8-12. Warning: you are about to do something important!

Now you can open the *Code.gs* file and add the final nail to this app's coffin. Way back at the beginning of this chapter the Earth was empty, a formless mass cloaked in darkness... Wait, wrong book. The point is, there was nothing in the DB, so to reset the app we need to again make the DB empty. You may actually find this function quite handy anytime you need to clear out a ScriptDB:

```
function reset(){
  var db = ScriptDb.getMyDb();
  while (true) {
    var result = db.query({});
    if (result.getSize() == 0) {
      break;
    }
    while (result.hasNext()) {
      db.remove(result.next());
    }
  }
}
```

 If you do clear your ScriptDB, there is no way to recover it. Put another way, the contents are gone forever and ever and ever. Always be very careful when running operations like this. If there is any question that you may need to recover, include some sort of output before clearing the DB.

The testing you have done so far needs to be deleted so we can start fresh. Go ahead and click the big red button so you can ensure that the app is completed.

Deploying Using Add-ons

The newest thing to hit the Google Apps Script shelves is a feature called *Add-ons* (*http://bit.ly/google-addon*) (see Figure 8-13). What Add-ons will let you do is distribute container-bound apps like the one in this chapter to every Google Apps user through a new Add-ons menu in Google Docs, Sheets, and Forms. Keep an eye out for a book by this author that will walk you through all the steps of deploying your Google Apps Script applications using Add-ons or the Google Chrome Web Store.

Figure 8-13. Add-ons

Finishing Up

This has been a long chapter and a large app to sink your teeth into. Hopefully you now have a good grasp on how to not only work within a container but also use valuable services like ScriptDB to store information. If nothing else, I'm sure you have taken away a firm understanding of client/server iteration.

Full Code

You can find all of the code for the files below on this book's Google Drive (*http://bit.ly/ch8-code*).

Code for *Code.gs*.

```
var ui = DocumentApp.getUi();

function onOpen() {
  ui
      .createMenu('Approvals')
      .addItem('Approve/Reject Request', 'approveRejectRequest')
      .addItem('Start Workflow', 'startWorkflow')
      .addItem('Approval Status', 'approvalStatus')
      .addItem('View History', 'viewHistory')
      .addItem('Reset Workflow', 'resetWorkflow')
      .addToUi();
}
```

```
function startWorkflow() {
  var html = HtmlService.createTemplateFromFile('startWorkflow').evaluate()
      .setTitle('Start Workflow').setWidth(300)
      .setSandboxMode(HtmlService.SandboxMode.NATIVE);
  ui.showSidebar(html);
}

function approveRejectRequest() {
   var html = HtmlService.createTemplateFromFile('ApproveRejectRequest').evalu-
ate()
      .setTitle('Approve/Reject Request').setWidth(300)
      .setSandboxMode(HtmlService.SandboxMode.NATIVE);
  ui.showSidebar(html);
}

function approvalStatus() {
  var html = HtmlService.createTemplateFromFile('ApprovalStatus').evaluate()
    .setTitle('Approval Status').setWidth(300)
    .setSandboxMode(HtmlService.SandboxMode.NATIVE);
  ui.showSidebar(html);
}

function viewHistory() {
  var html = HtmlService.createTemplateFromFile('ViewHistory').evaluate()
      .setTitle('View History').setWidth(300)
      .setSandboxMode(HtmlService.SandboxMode.NATIVE);
  ui.showSidebar(html);
}

function resetWorkflow() {
  var html = HtmlService.createTemplateFromFile('ResetWorkflow').evaluate()
      .setTitle('Reset Workflow').setWidth(300)
      .setSandboxMode(HtmlService.SandboxMode.NATIVE);
  ui.showSidebar(html);
}

/**
 * This function will create a new entry in the DB with default values
 * @param {String} email The email address for the user you want to add
 * @returns {String} 201 Created, 409 Conflict, 500 Internal Server Error
 */
function addApprover(email){
  var db = ScriptDb.getMyDb();
  var docId = DocumentApp.getActiveDocument().getId();
  var ob =      {
                docId: docId,
                approverEmail: email,
                status: null,
                emailSent: false
```

```
              }
    db.save(ob);

    var history =  {
              docId: docId,
              action: 'Added Approver',
              email: email,
                date: Utilities.formatDate(new Date(), "GMT", "MM-dd-yyyy'
'HH:mm:ss"),
              }
    db.save(history);
}

/**
 * This function will remove an approver from the DB
 * @param {String} email The email address for the user you want to delete
 * @returns {String} 200 OK, 500 Internal Server Error
 */
function removeApprover(email){
    var docId = DocumentApp.getActiveDocument().getId();
    var db = ScriptDb.getMyDb();
    var result = db.query({docId: docId, approverEmail: email});
    db.remove(result.next());

    var history =  {
              docId: docId,
              action: 'Removed Approver',
              email: email,
                date: Utilities.formatDate(new Date(), "GMT", "MM-dd-yyyy'
'HH:mm:ss"),
              }
    db.save(history);
}

/**
 * This function will return a list of approver objects in the db
 * @returns {Object Array} [{status:null,emailSent:true}, ...]
 */
function getApprovers(){
    var docId = DocumentApp.getActiveDocument().getId();
    var db = ScriptDb.getMyDb();
    var result = db.query({docId: docId, approverEmail: db.anyValue()});
    var approvers =[];
    while (result.hasNext()) {
      approvers.push(result.next());
    }
    Logger.log(approvers)
    return approvers;
}
```

```
/**
 * This function will retrieve a single approver from the DB
 * @param {String} email The email address for the user
 * @returns {Object} The Approver Object or null if not found
 */
function getApprover(email){
  var docId = DocumentApp.getActiveDocument().getId();
  var db = ScriptDb.getMyDb();
  var result = db.query({docId: docId, approverEmail: email});
  return result.next();
}

/**
 * This function will change an approver's Status
 * @param {String} email The email address for the user
 * @returns {Object} The Approver Object or null if not found
 */
function setApproverStatus(email, status){
  var docId = DocumentApp.getActiveDocument().getId();
  var db = ScriptDb.getMyDb();
  var ob = db.query({docId: docId, approverEmail: email}).next();
  if (ob == null)return;
  ob.status = status;
  db.save(ob);

  var history =  {
            docId: docId,
            action: 'Changed Status to: '+status,
            email: email,
              date: Utilities.formatDate(new Date(), "GMT", "MM-dd-yyyy'
'HH:mm:ss"),
          }
  db.save(history);
}

function getHistory(){
  var docId = DocumentApp.getActiveDocument().getId();
  var db = ScriptDb.getMyDb();
  var result = db.query({docId: docId, action: db.anyValue()});
  var history =[];
  while (result.hasNext()) {
    history.push(result.next());
  }
  var sorted = history.sort(function(a, b) {
  return a.date.replace(/[^0-9.]/g, "") - b.date.replace(/[^0-9.]/g, "")});
  return sorted.reverse();
}

function reset(){
    var db = ScriptDb.getMyDb();
    while (true) {
      var result = db.query({});
```

```
      if (result.getSize() == 0) {
        break;
      }
      while (result.hasNext()) {
        db.remove(result.next());
      }
    }
  }
}

function start(){
  var docId = DocumentApp.getActiveDocument().getId();
  var db = ScriptDb.getMyDb();
  var result = db.query({docId: docId, approverEmail: db.anyValue()});
  while (result.hasNext()) {
    var record = result.next();
    if(record.status == null){
      var doc = DocumentApp.getActiveDocument();
      doc.addEditor(record.approverEmail);
      var url = doc.getUrl();

      MailApp.sendEmail({
           to: record.approverEmail,
           subject: "Please Review my Document",
           htmlBody: 'You have been asked to review and approve '+
           'a document<br>Please <a href="'+url+'">Click here</a> '+
           'to Open the document.<br><br>'+
           'After reviewing click the Approvals menu and select '+
           'Approve/Reject Request',
      });

      record.status = 'Email Sent'
      db.save(record);
    }
  }
}

function sendReminder(approverEmail){
  MailApp.sendEmail({
           to: approverEmail,
           subject: "Please Review my Document",
           htmlBody: 'You have been asked to review and approve '+
           'a document<br>Please <a href="'+
           DocumentApp.getActiveDocument().getUrl()+'">
               Click here</a> to Open the document.<br><br>'+
               'After reviewing click the Approvals menu and '+
               'select Approve/Reject Request',
  });
}
```

Code for *ApproveRejectRequest.html.*

```html
<div id="wrapper">
  <div>
    <span>You have been asked to approve this document.
    Please select your approval type from the list below.
    Clicking the Submit button will confirm your choice and
    notify the document owner. </span>
  </div>
  <div>
    <br>
    <select id="status">
      <option>Select Approval Type</option>
      <option>Approve &amp; No Edits</option>
      <option>Approve &amp; Allow Edits</option>
      <option>Needs Work</option>
      <option>Delegate</option>
      <option>Doesn't Need My Approval</option>
      <option>Rejected</option>
    </select>
  </div>
    <br>

  <div class="center">
    <span id="submitButton" class="button redButton">Submit</span>
  </div>
</div>

<?!= HtmlService.createHtmlOutputFromFile('styles').getContent(); ?>
<script src="http://ajax.googleapis.com/ajax/libs/jquery/1.8.3/jquery.min.js">
</script>

<script>
    $(document).ready(function() {
      $('#submitButton').click(submit);

      google.script.run.withSuccessHandler(function(approvers) {
        var notListed = true;
        var user = <?=Session.getEffectiveUser().getEmail()?>;
        for(var i =0; i < approvers.length; i++){
          if(user.toLowerCase() == approvers[i].approverEmail
            .toLowerCase()){
            notListed = false;
            break;
          }
        }
        if(notListed){
          $('#wrapper').html('You are not an approver for this Document.')
        }
      }).getApprovers();

    });
```

```
        function submit(){
          var email = <?=Session.getEffectiveUser().getEmail()?>;
          var status = $('#status').val();
          google.script.run.withSuccessHandler(function() {
            $('#wrapper').html('Your Approval Status has been recorded.')
          }).setApproverStatus(email, status);
        }

  </script>
```

Code for *startWorkflow.html.*

```
<div id="wrapper">
  <div>
    <span>Let's get started with your workflow. First add an approver
    by entering their email address in the Approvers box and clicking
    the add button. When you are done adding approvers, click the
    Start Workflow button.</span>
  </div>
  <br>
  <div>
    <span class="sectionHeader">Approvers</span><br>
    <div id="approvers">
    </div>
    <div>
      <form id="addApprover">
        <input type="email" id="approver" placeholder="Email Address">
        <input type="submit" class="button blueButton" value="Add">
      </form>
    </div>
  </div>
  <br>
  <div class="center">
    <span id="startButton" class="button redButton">Start Workflow</span>
  </div>
</div>

<?!= HtmlService.createHtmlOutputFromFile('styles').getContent(); ?>
<script src="http://ajax.googleapis.com/ajax/libs/jquery/1.8.3/jquery.min.js">
</script>

<script>
      $(document).ready(function() {
        //bind click handlers at runtime
        $('#addApprover').submit(addApprover);
        $('#startButton').click(startWorkflow);
        getApprovers();

      });

      function addApprover(){
        google.script.run.withSuccessHandler(function() {
```

```
            getApprovers();
            $('#approver').val('');
          }).addApprover($("#approver").val());
        }

        function getApprovers(){
          google.script.run.withSuccessHandler(function(approvers) {
            $("#approvers").html('');
            for(var i =0; i < approvers.length; i++){
              $("#approvers").append(
                '<img class="approver" email="'+approvers[i].approverEmail+'"'
                title="Click to remove this Approver"'+
        'src="https://googledrive.com/host/0B61-C9Nl4dO-ZEpvTk9SWU5tYnc/x_ico1.png"
        width="12px"><span> '+approvers[i].approverEmail+'</span><br>'
              );
            }
            $('.approver').on('click', function() {
              removeApprover($(this).attr('email'));
            });
          }).getApprovers();
        }

        function removeApprover(approver){
          google.script.run.withSuccessHandler(function() {
            getApprovers();
          }).removeApprover(approver);
        }

        function startWorkflow(){
          google.script.run.withSuccessHandler(function() {
            $('#wrapper').html('OK, I have sent emails to the approvers.
            <br>You can see their responses from the Approval Status menu.')
          }).start();
        }
    </script>
```

Code for *ApprovalStatus.html.*

```
<div id="wrapper">
  <br>

  <div>
    <span class="sectionHeader">Awaiting Approval</span><br>
    <div class="spaceAfter" id="notApproved"></div>
  </div>
  <br>
  <hr>
  <div>
    <span class="sectionHeader">Approvers with Response</span><br>
    <div id="responded"></div>
  </div>
  <br>
  <br>
```

```
  <div>
  Approvers can be added to or removed from the Start Workflow menu.
  </div>
</div>


<?!= HtmlService.createHtmlOutputFromFile('styles').getContent(); ?>
<script src="http://ajax.googleapis.com/ajax/libs/jquery/1.8.3/jquery.min.js">
</script>

<script>
    $(document).ready(function() {
      loadApproverStatus(); //loads the approvers from the data store
    });

    /**
     * This function sends a server request to get the list of approvers
     * @returns null This function loads the UI directly after
     *   processing server call
     */
    function loadApproverStatus(){
      google.script.run.withSuccessHandler(function(approvers) {
        for(var i =0; i < approvers.length; i++){
          if(approvers[i].status == null ||
          approvers[i].status =='Email Sent'){
            $("#notApproved").append('<span class="approverEmail red"> '+
            approvers[i].approverEmail+' </span>'+
            '<span class="reminder" email="'+approvers[i].approverEmail+
            '">Send Reminder</span><br>');
          }else{
            $("#responded").append('<span class="approverEmail green"> '+
            approvers[i].approverEmail+'</span><br>'+
              '<span class="status spaceAfter"">'+approvers[i].status+
              '</span><br>');
          }
        }
        $('.reminder').on('click', function() { //adds a click handler to
                                                //each Send Reminder button
          sendReminder($(this).attr('email'));
          $(this).text('Sent');
        });
      }).getApprovers();
    }

    /**
     * This function sends a server request to send a reminder email
     * @param {String} approver The email address for the user
     */
    function sendReminder(approver){
      google.script.run.withSuccessHandler(function() {
      }).sendReminder(approver);
```

```
    }
  </script>
```

Code for *ViewHistory.html*.

```html
<div id="wrapper">
<div>
  <span>These are the actions that have been taken.</span>
</div>

<br>

  <div>
    <div id="approvers"></div>
  </div>
</div>

<?!= HtmlService.createHtmlOutputFromFile('styles').getContent(); ?>
<script src="http://ajax.googleapis.com/ajax/libs/jquery/1.8.3/jquery.min.js">
</script>

<script>
    $(document).ready(function() {
      google.script.run.withSuccessHandler(function(history) {
        $("#approvers").html('');
        for(var i =0; i < history.length; i++){
        $("#approvers").append(
          '<span class="sectionHeader">'+history[i].date+'</span><br>'+
          '<span class="approverEmail">'+history[i].email+'</span><br>'+
          '<span class="status">'+history[i].action+'</span><br>'+
          '<hr>'
        );

        }
      }).getHistory();
    });
</script>
```

Code for *ResetWorkflow.html*.

```html
<div id="wrapper" class="center">
  <div>
    <span class="warning">Warning!</span><br>
    <span>You are about to reset this workflow. Clicking the Reset
    button will erase all approval history and approvers.</span>
  </div>
  <br>
  <br>
  <div>
    You can close this window to cancel the reset.<br><br>
    <span id="resetButton" class="button redButton">Confirm Reset</span>
  </div>
</div>
```

```
<?!= HtmlService.createHtmlOutputFromFile('styles').getContent(); ?>
<script src="http://ajax.googleapis.com/ajax/libs/jquery/1.8.3/jquery.min.js">
</script>

<script>
    $(document).ready(function() {
      $('#resetButton').click(resetWorkflow);
    });

    function resetWorkflow(){
      google.script.run.withSuccessHandler(function() {
        $('#wrapper').html('<h3>The Workflow has been reset</h3>');
      }).reset();
    }
</script>
```

Code for *styles.html.*

```
<style type="text/css">

.sectionHeader {
  color: #202020 ;
  font-size: 18px;
  text-decoration:underline;
  margin-bottom: 20px;
}

.button {
  color: #FFFFFF;
  font-size: 12px;
  moz-border-radius: 3px;
  -webkit-border-radius: 3px;
  padding: 3px;
  border:0;
}

.blueButton {
  background-color: #3366FF;
}

.redButton {
  background-color: #C80000;
}

.button:hover{
  opacity:0.7;
}

.center {
  text-align: center;
}

#wrapper {
```

```
    margin:2px 4px 3px 4px;
    font-family: Verdana, Geneva, sans-serif;
}

.reminder {
    color: #FFFFFF;
    background-color: #3366FF;
    font-size: 10px;
    moz-border-radius: 3px;
    -webkit-border-radius: 3px;
    padding: 3px;
}

.approverEmail {
    font-size: 12px;
    margin-left: 10px;
    color: #383838;
}

.approverEmail.red {
    color: #C80000;
}

.approverEmail.green {
    color: #009900;
}

.status {
    color: #686868;
    font-size: 12px;
    margin-left: 25px;
}

.spaceAfter {
    line-height: 25px;
}

.warning {
    color: #C80000;
    font-size: 24px;
}
</style>
```

CHAPTER 9

Mashup

In this last chapter, we will build smaller apps that help your users do more with Google. One of the most requested scripts we hear about is from the IT admin who has his hands full keeping the router up and running but now also needs to help get the Google website's forms submitted to the right department. To take care of this task, we will cover automating the sending of emails to different people when Google forms are submitted.

Oh and don't forget, the boss also likes to see pretty charts to demonstrate how well her department is performing, and that information needs to be a live update. Google Sites allows you to organize data and create great reports and in this chapter you will learn how to get data from a spreadsheet and display it as a chart that dazzles your boos and gets you that raise we know you deserve.

Directing Email Using Google Forms

Google Forms are a very convenient way to quickly get information into a spreadsheet. Add some Google Apps Scripts, and you can turbocharge those forms to send email notifications, generate other data in the spreadsheet, and do lots of other things you might want to do when getting data from a form.

In this section you will learn the basics of getting form information into a Google Apps Script and sending an email based on a selection from a drop down-list in the Google Form.

Here are the tools you'll be using:

- Google Forms
- MailApp
- Event triggers

Open a Google spreadsheet and start creating a form. The example we will use is for routing inquiries to the right department: sales or service. Figure 9-1 shows the form editor and the drop-down box selection.

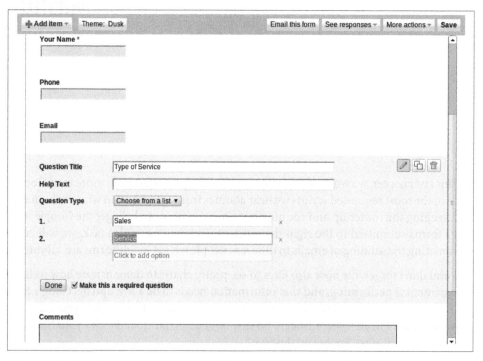

Figure 9-1. Google Forms can be inserted into most websites and emailed

After creating the form you can return to the spreadsheet, where you'll see that the form fields have become columns (see Figure 9-2).

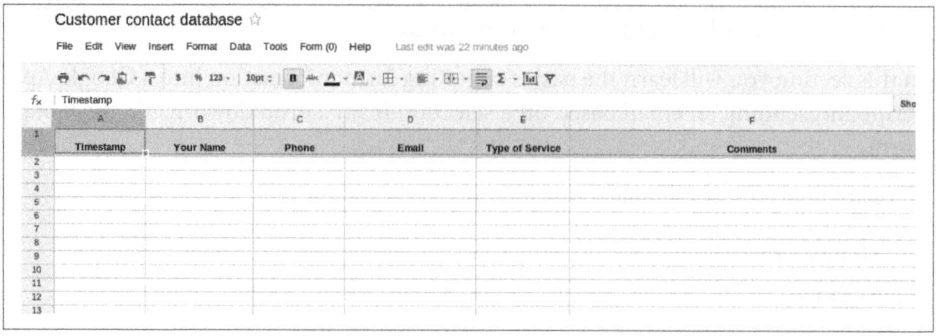

Figure 9-2. Note that the timestamp is automatically added

Now open the Script Editor (Tools→"Script editor").

You can delete the default function and start the script with global variables (outside any function) that will contain the email addresses for the two departments:

```
var sales = 'sales@example.com';
var service = 'service@example.com';
//add more as needed
```

Now create a `notify` function that will be used to send the emails. Don't forget the e parameter, which will be used later in this section to pass form-submit values.

Create a variable to hold the selected department. Next, add a JavaScript `switch`, which is much more efficient in this case than stacking `if` statements.

The `switch` argument is where we need to get the value from the form when it is submitted. These values are passed in the parameter e.values, which is a zero-based array that looks like this: `["2011/11/17 13:00", "James", "555-5555", "customer@gmail.com", "Sales", "comments"]`. As you may have guessed, the spreadsheet columns line up with these values in a zero-based array.

 If you get confused about which number in the array lines up with a certain form field, just count from the top on the form. The timestamp, which is not on the form, is always in e.values[0].

Looking at the form, location 4 is the listbox containing the department. Use this in the `switch` arguments. In a `switch`, you use cases with the values you hope to match. Yes, they are case-sensitive, if you were wondering. All that needs to be done for this simple script is to set the value of `email` to the correct department variable. Don't forget to `break`; at the end of each case, or you will run the next case as well:

```
function notify(e) {
  var email = '';

  switch (e.values[4]){

        case 'Sales':
          email = sales;
        break;

        case 'Service':
          email = service;
        break;
  }
```

When sending an email to the correct department, it would be great to also add the details of the request so they don't need to go to the spreadsheet. You can use HTML in the body of the messages you send, which helps you to make a nice presentation for your staff.

Simply add your field variables to the correct places in the HTML template. If you would like a more complex template, consider using a template file and key values, as described in Chapter 6:

```
var html =
    '<body>'+
    '<h2>Please contact: '+ e.values[1] +'</h2>'+
    'Comment: <br />'+
    e.values[5] + '<br />'+
    '<br />'+
    'Phone: ' + e.values[2] + '<br />'+
    'Email: ' + e.values[3] + '<br />'+
    '</body>';
```

All that is left is to send the email using the MailApp Service. To customize the subject, add the type of request using `e.values[4]` in the second argument:

```
MailApp.sendEmail(email, "Information Request: "+e.values[4] ,
'No plain text body );',
{htmlBody: html});
}
```

Save the script and run it once to grant permission for MailApp. Now that the form and script are ready, it is time to set up a form-submit trigger. In the menu, click Triggers→ "Current script triggers," and in the pop-up window, select "Click here to add one now."

Figure 9-3 shows the triggers dialog box, where you will need to select the `notify` function and "On form submit" from the listboxes. Click Save.

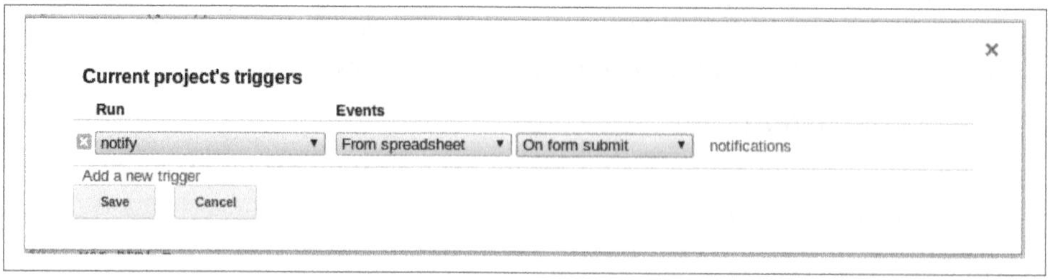

Figure 9-3. You can also set time-based triggers here

Once again you have added tremendous functionality to your business website and made the boss proud; certainly you deserve a raise. You can now go to the live web form and make a submission to check that an email was delivered to the correct department.

This has been a basic example of working with these different services; however, much more can be done in the processing here. For example, if you have existing customers somewhere in a database, the script could pull that information and include it in the email, kick off a workflow from Chapter 8, or even send you a text message if the mail is from a really important client.

Charts in Sites

Charts are an important way to convey information to coworkers, stakeholders, and even the general public. Built into Google Apps Script is a complete chart-making service that parallels what is available in the Google Sheets Service.

In this section we will look at two charts: one generated from stock information and a second from a spreadsheet. The script will be created as a standalone service so it can be available in the browser as a single page or inserted in your Google Site as a gadget.

FinanceApp Chart

Maybe you work for a company that has a public stock and you want to display it on your page, or maybe you're a trader who needs to quickly display historical stock data from your phone; in any case, Google Apps Script lets you get that data and dress it up in a nice graphical chart.

Pop open a new script, create a file, and name it "Finance." This will hold the code for retrieving the information from the Finance Service and building a data table used by the Charts Service to make a graphic.

For purposes of example, this function will return the past year's worth of weekly quotes when given a stock symbol.

The end date is today, `newDate()`, so when your page is loaded two months from now it will be updated to the latest information with no effort on your part. It takes a few more methods to tease out the start date, but it is exactly one year before the current date. Just remember the direction: start is not from now until then; rather, it's from that time in the past until now.

`FinanceApp.getHistoricalStockInfo` will return an array of quote objects given the time frame. In the arguments we specify the symbol, start date, and end date. The last parameter is the interval in days that you would like to sample, with 7 meaning every week.

You will need to create a `dataTable` object from the Charts Service and add columns for month and price. Note that the type of data must be set for each column.

The quotes array is in the parameter `stockInfo`, so we call that into a variable `quotes` to avoid typing it all out every time. We iterate through the quotes array, adding a row to the `dataTable` for each entry. Arguments in the `addRow` method are in the same order as the columns added to the `dataTable`. The `Utilities.formatDate` method with an

"MMM" argument gets us just the month for the quote, to save some space on the chart. The second argument in the addRow method is the closing price.

Finally, we issue dataTable.build and return the dataTable. The complete code is shown here:

```
/*
 *  Builds the chart dataTable from a stock symbol
 *
 *  Arguments:
 *  Name          Type      Description
 *  stockSymbol   string    a valid stock symbol, ie goog
 *
 *  returns DataTable()
 */
function buildFromFinance(stockSymbol) {

   var endDate = new Date();
   var startDate = new Date(new Date(endDate)
   .setFullYear(endDate.getFullYear()-1));
   var stockHist = FinanceApp.getHistoricalStockInfo(stockSymbol,
   startDate, endDate, 7);

   var dataTable = Charts.newDataTable();
   dataTable.addColumn(Charts.ColumnType.STRING, 'Month');
   dataTable.addColumn(Charts.ColumnType.NUMBER, 'Price');

   var quotes = stockHist.stockInfo;
   for (var i in stockHist.stockInfo)

     dataTable.addRow([Utilities
         .formatDate(new Date(stockHist.stockInfo[i].time),
                     "EST", "MMM"), stockHist.stockInfo[i].close]);

   dataTable.build();
   return dataTable;
 }
```

Now that we have a dataTable loaded with a year's worth of stock quotes, we just need to plug the table into a chart.

Go to the *Code.gs* file and start the standalone UI function.

The first variable is the symbol, which we make static here, but if you want to jazz things up, you can add a listbox or other way for the user to choose a certain quote. Next, the dataTable is built using the function you created before. There are several set parameters to allow you to customize the chart, but the most important steps are: plugging in the data using the setDataTable method and issuing the build command:

```
function doGet() {

  var app = UiApp.createApplication().setTitle("Stock Chart");
```

```
    var symbol = 'goog';
    var data = buildFromFinance(symbol);

    var chart = Charts.newLineChart()
        .setDimensions(600, 300)
        .setDataTable(data)
        .setColors(['#006400'])
        .setBackgroundColor('transparent')
        .setCurveStyle(Charts.CurveStyle.SMOOTH)
        .setTitle('Last 12 Months for '+symbol.toUpperCase())
        .build();

    var title = app.createLabel('Custom Stock Quotes');

    //style goes here

    app.add(chart);
    app.add(title);

    return app;
}
```

Add the chart and title to the app, and you are ready to publish the page. Figure 9-4 shows the published page loaded in a new browser window. It looks good, but we can make it better with the power of CSS.

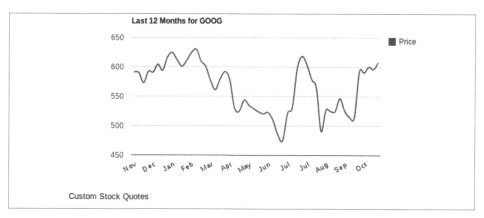

Figure 9-4. You can put these in an email as well

Open a new file, and name it "CSS." You will need a function to apply the CSS and three objects holding the style attributes:

```
function applyCSS_(element, style){
  for (var key in style){
    element.setStyleAttribute(key, style[key]);
  }
}
```

```
var _background =
    {
    "position":"fixed",
    "top":"0px",
    "left":"0px"
    }

var _chart =
    {
    "position":"fixed",
    "top":"0px",
    "left":"0px"
    }

var _title =
    {
    "position":"fixed",
    "top":"265px",
    "left":"30px",
    "color":"#0000FF",
    "font-size":"24",
    "font-family":"cursive,Times New Roman"
    }
```

Using the `"position":"fixed"` parameter frees widgets from inlining and allows you to stack them on top of each other.

The order that widgets stack is determined by when they are added on the page. The first thing added is at the bottom.

Go back to the *Code.gs* file and add the formatting at the place marker. Choose an image for the background, and load it on the app as the bottom item:

```
var background = app.createImage('https://5079980847011989849-a-'+
    '1802744773732722657-s-sites.googlegroups.com/site/scriptsexamples/'+
    'WallSt%281%29.png');
background.setSize('600px', '300px');
app.add(background);
applyCSS_(background, _background);
applyCSS_(title, _title);
applyCSS_(chart, _chart);
```

Apply the CSS to the widgets, save, and reload the published page. The result is shown in Figure 9-5.

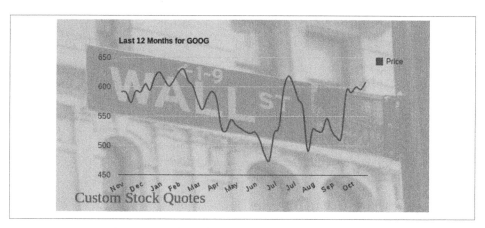

Figure 9-5. CSS makes an OK chart dazzle

Chart from a Spreadsheet

Wouldn't it be great to have a spreadsheet with all your data that automatically generates charts on your Google Site? If that sort of thing is for you, read on: this section will show you how amazingly easy it is to write a script that can be used on most any spreadsheet that you want to generate a chart.

The first thing you need is some data and a spreadsheet. In your spreadsheet, make the normal header section in row 1 to identify each column. In row 2, you will need to identify what kind of value that column contains: string, number, etc. (see Figure 9-6).

Spreadsheet

Month	In Store	Online
String	Number	Number
Jan	10	1
Feb	12	1
Mar	20	2
Apr	21	7
May	15	20

chart

Figure 9-6. Row 2 can easily be added to spreadsheets fed by a form

As in the Finance chart in the last section, a function will be used to create the data table.

In the *Code.gs* file add the function `buildFromSpreadsheet`, which takes an argument that is a range of spreadsheet values created by the `getValues` method from SpreadsheetApp.

Create a `data-Table` object and then start iterating the values in `range[0]`, which is row 1, where the headers are. These values are added to the data table as columns. `range[1]` is row 2 and is used in the first argument of `.addColumn` to set the column types.

The next `for` loop starts on row 3, in the array index 2, and adds each row. The argument for `addRow` is comma-separated by column values, which is how each row is formatted in `range[i]`.

Build the data table and return it:

```
function buildFromSpreadsheet(range){
  var dataTable = Charts.newDataTable();

  for (var j in range[0]) //create the columns
    dataTable.addColumn(Charts.ColumnType[range[1][j].toUpperCase()],
    range[0][j]);

  for (var i=2; i< range.length; i++) //create the rows
    dataTable.addRow(range[i]);

  dataTable.build();

  return dataTable;
}
```

To use this new function, you will get the data range as values from the spreadsheet. This example uses `getDataRange`, but you can also use any of the other range calls as long as the first two rows match the header/column type scheme.

After `buildFromSpreadsheet` returns your data table, you are ready to build the chart object. This one is an area chart and has only a few settings to consider. Setting the range will help the readability, and the title will tell the user what it is:

```
function doGet() {

  var range = SpreadsheetApp.openById('<YOUR Spreadsheet ID>')
              .getSheetByName('chart').getDataRange().getValues();

  var data = buildFromSpreadsheet(range);

  var chart = Charts.newAreaChart()
      .setDataTable(data)
      .setStacked()
      .setRange(0, 40)
      .setTitle("Sales per Month")
      .build();
```

```
var app = UiApp.createApplication().setTitle("My Chart");
app.add(chart);

return uiApp;
}
```

Create a UiApp instance and add the chart. Publish the script and load up the page. Figure 9-7 shows the final product. A simple, non-CSS version like this can work very well inline on a Google Sites page.

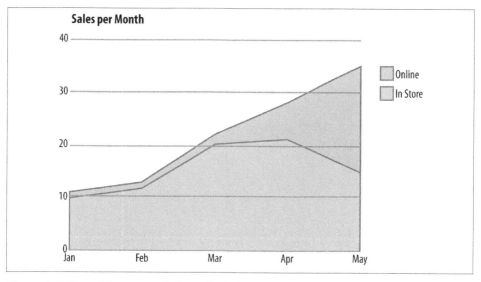

Figure 9-7. Try adding several charts built from one set of data

Index

A

Add-ons feature, 171
addEmail function, 45
application canvas, 103
approvers
    adding, 152
    loading, 153
    removing, 155
arrays
    2D, 49
    converted to objects, 115
    zero-based, 48, 63
audit logs, 153, 166
authorization, 11, 87

B

<body> tags, 36, 86
branding, 104
breaking the code, 27
breaks, 26
buttons, 41

C

callbacks, 43
camelCase, 63, 115
catalogs, 53
changes, saving, 127

charts
    chart-making services, 187
    generated from data, 187
    generated from spreadsheets, 191
client-side handlers, 118
client_id value, 114
client_secret value, 114
Cloud Console, 113
clutter, 53
Contact Me form
    adding style with CSS, 37
    building the UI, 35
    data storage, 46
    functions, 46
    handling user actions, 42–45
container-bound apps
    UI creation with HTML Service, 14
    UI creation with UiApp Service, 11
    vs. web apps, 23
content area, 108
controls component, 107
Create menu, 17
createDoc function, 92
createHtmlOutputFromFile(<FileName>), 34
createTemplateFromFile(<FileName>), 34
createWebPage method, 63
customer experience
    limiting page clutter, 53
    mouseovers vs. page changes, 57

We'd like to hear your suggestions for improving our indexes. Send email to index@oreilly.com.

product information, 56

D

data storage
  choices for, 46
  data set up for, 49
  file cabinet pages, 56
  Google's Cloud SQL, 151
  image repositories, 56
    available systems, 55
    database loading, 57
    database set up, 56
    file cabinet pages for, 56
    image dimensions/descriptions, 56
  installed applications vs. web-based, 99
  ScriptDB, 151
  spreadsheet set up for, 47
  UiApp-style database application
    benefits of, 100
    deleting records, 131
    editing records, 125
    foundation for, 103–109
    full code for, 132
    Fusion Tables, 112–118
    inserting records, 128
    overview of, 100
    saving changes, 127
    search view, 109–112
    set up for, 102
    viewing records, 119–125
debugging
  break and report, 27
  Debug button, 10
  during development, 25
  errors and breaks, 26
  Execution Transcript, 8
  production error logging, 28
  syntax checking, 26
development environment
  debugging/testing, 26
  IDE look for, 25
  production error logging, 28
Docs Picker, 87
document workflows, 141
  (see also email document workflow app)
doGet function
  as starting point, 33
  for Google URL, 17
  granting permission, 29

special status of, 16, 144
when to use, 46
doPost function
  special status of, 16, 144
  when to use, 46

E

Eclipse, 4
Edit menu, 7
elements, 33, 43
email document workflow app
  approval status, 162
  audit history, 166
  benefits of, 142
  deployment with Add-ons, 171
  full code for, 171
  menu creation, 143
  overview of, 143
  recording approvals, 158
  reset feature, 168
  sidebar loading, 145
  Start Workflow operation
    adding approvers, 152
    JavaScript for, 150
    loading approvers, 153
    removing approvers, 155
    ScriptDB data storage, 151
    start button click handler, 156
    startWorkflow.html, 147
email notifications
  adding details to, 186
  basic set up for, 184
  trigger set up, 186
  using Google Forms, 183
error messages
  Authorization is required…, 29, 87
  TypeError:Failed due to illegal value…, 31
errors
  Fusion Table configuration, 112
  in callbacks, 44
  production error logging, 28
  runtime, 26
  try/catch statement, 26
Execution Transcript, 8

F

file cabinet pages, 56
File menu, 6

FinanceApp chart, 187
find/replace, 7
Flex Tables, 110, 117
forms
    automatic creation of, 82
    element layout in, 119
    Forms feature, 81, 183
    response forms, 35
functions
    basic types of, 46
    hiding from Run menu, 102
    naming of, 16, 144
Fusion Tables
    client-side handlers, 118
    configuring access to, 112
    creation of, 111
    customization of, 111
    database application, 100
    getting data from, 114
    loading data in UI, 115

G

Gadgets, 21, 68
getActiveApplication function, 105
getElementById function, 110
getImages function, 70
getRange method, 48
getSheetByName function, 69
getSheets function, 69
getSheets method, 48
global variables, 85, 102
Gmail, 142
Google App Engine, 4
Google Apps Script
    basics of
        advantages of, 3, 5
        getting started, 5
        Manage Versions feature, 6, 18
        script editor, 6
        UI creation methods, 10
        UI creation with Google Sites, 21
        UI creation with HTML Service, 4, 14
        UI creation with UiApp Service, 4
        UI creation with web apps, 16
    building a web app UI
        callbacks, 43
        Contact Me form example, 35
        data storage, 46–49
        doGet function, 33

elements of, 33
    functions, 46
    handler anatomy, 42
    handling user actions, 41
        (see also data storage)
development environment
    debugging/testing, 26
    IDE look for, 25
    production error logging, 28
hiding functions from Run menu, 102
open-source libraries for, 60
Scriptlet language, 68
Google Chrome Web Store, 9
Google Cloud Console, 113
Google Docs
    Add-ons feature, 171
    form tool, 35
    in document workflow, 142
    Sidebar feature, 14, 145
    templates in, 81
    unique IDs, 48
Google Drawings, 103
Google Drive service, 5, 100
Google Forms, 81, 183
Google Script Editor
    accessing common tasks, 10
    Edit menu, 7
    File menu, 6
    Find Selection, 7
    project creation in, 5
    Project properties, 7
    Publish menu, 9
    publishing options, 18
    Resources menu, 9
    saving scripts, 6
    securing code with sharing, 23
    View menu, 8
Google Sheets, 81
Google Sites, 21, 59, 62
Google Web Toolkit (GWT), 4
google.script.run, 31, 46
Google's Cloud SQL, 151
grids, 104, 106, 108
.gs files, 14
GUI Builder, 103

H

handlers
    client-side, 41, 118

UiApp page loading and, 105
values passed by, 109
<head> tags, 36
headers grid, 104
hover display
    adding, 73
    opacity effect, 148
    pop-up panels, 53
    product information, 57
    selectable items, 118
    user interaction through, 41
HTML Service, 4, 14, 37
HTML5 email validation, 148

I

ID values, 121
image file repository
    available systems, 55
    database loading, 57
    database set up, 56
    file cabinet pages for, 56
    image dimensions/descriptions, 56

J

JavaScript
    camelCase text, 63
    in email document workflows, 150
    top-down language of, 102
    zero-based arrays in, 48, 63
JavaScript objects, 60
jQuery, 42, 59

K

key-value pairs, 7, 115
keys, 82, 89

L

libraries
    adding, 9, 60
    creating, 10, 60
    open-source, 60
links, 104
listBox widget, 123
Logger Service, 8
logos, 104
logs
    audit, 153, 166

backend, 28
HTML frontend, 29

M

magnifying glass icon, 106
Manage Versions feature, 6, 18
mobile apps, 100
mouse handlers, 41, 73, 118
multiple panels, working with, 103
multiple-choice questions, 91

N

name values, 121
nonprinting scriptlets, 37

O

ObjApp library, 63, 89
off handler, 41
onChange handler, 41
onEdit function, 16, 144
onFormSubmit function, 144
onInstall function, 16, 144
onOpen function, 16, 144
.openById, 48
.openByUrl, 48
over handler, 41

P

page clutter, 53
panels
    headers grid, 104
    logo placement, 104
    main panel, 103
    pop-up panels, 53
permissions, 19, 29
printing scriptlets, 37
Product version box, 18
production error logging
    backend logging, 28
    logging HTML frontends, 29
Production Link, 20
progress indicators, 41
Project properties, 7
Properties option, 7
Properties Service, 7
publishing options, 18

R

random numbers, 58
rangeToObjects, 115
records
    custom formatting, 122
    deleting, 131
    editing, 125
    fetching, 119
    inserting new, 128
    listBox formatting, 123
    searching, 105, 109
    viewing, 119, 121
Resources menu, 9
response forms, 35
Revisions box, 6
RPC (Remote Procedure Call), 43
Run menu, 102
runtime errors, 26

S

Script Editor
    accessing common tasks, 10
    Edit menu, 7
    File menu, 6
    Find Selection, 7
    project creation in, 5
    Project properties, 7
    Publish menu, 9
    publishing options, 18
    Resources menu, 9
    saving scripts, 6
    securing code with sharing, 23
    View menu, 8
Script icon, 17
Script Properties, 7
ScriptDB, 151
Scriptlet language, 68
scriptlets, 37, 69, 86
search component
    data store, 111
    loading, 105
    search view, 109
searchFusion(target, where) method, 114
security issues
    permissions, 19
    sharing in Script Editor, 23
setSandboxMode(HtmlService.Sandbox-
    Mode.NATIVE), 34, 145

Sharepoint, 141
Sidebar feature, 14, 145
smartphone displays, 100
Spreadsheet Service, 29, 69
spreadsheets
    benefits of, 57, 67
    chart generation from, 191
    creating pages from
        automated HTML filling, 59
        Google Apps Script objects class, 59
        JavaScript objects, 60
        open-source library installation, 60
        Sites Service for, 62
    data storage in, 47, 56
    directing email from, 184
    filling with Forms feature, 81
    filling with Sites Service, 62
    moving, 69
submit handler, 41
syntax errors, 26

T

tablet displays, 100
templates
    for project creation, 5
    generic vs. custom, 62
    in Google Docs, 81
    web app example
        basic, 83
        createDoc function, 92
        final code, 94
        form generation, 90
        form submission, 92
        functionality including, 82
        script creation, 84
        set up, 82
        template keys, 89
        template selection, 87
        UI creation, 85
triggers, 9, 186
try/catch statements, 26

U

UiApp (User Interface App) Service, 4, 11, 99
    (see also data storage)
UIs (user interfaces)
    creation methods, 10
    creation with Google Sites, 21

creation with HTML Service, 4
creation with UiApp Service, 4, 11
creation with web apps, 16
for product presentation
    as a gadget, 68
    features of, 67
    mouseover action, 73
    product display, 70
    user interaction, 72
unique IDs, 48, 58
user actions, 41
user experience
    fighting clutter with pop-up panels, 53
    interactive web pages, 76, 148
    viewing search results, 109

V

View menu, 8
visual product presentations
    application delivery, 77
    creating pages from spreadsheets
        automated HTML filling, 59
        Google Apps Script objects class, 59
        JavaScript objects, 60
        open-source library installation, 60
        Sites Service for, 62
    creating UI for
        as a gadget, 68

    features of, 67
    mouseover action, 73
    product display, 70
    user interaction, 72
    example of, 55
    image file repository
        available systems, 55
        database loading, 57
        database set up, 56
        file cabinet pages, 56
    importance of, 54
    limiting clutter with pop-up panels, 53
    optimized vs. traditional layouts, 54, 57

W

web pages
    eliminating clutter on, 54
        (see also visual product presentations)
    interactive, 76, 148
widgets, 4, 121
withFailureHandler, 44
withSuccessHandler, 45, 165

Y

YouTube App Library, 9

About the Author

James Ferreira managed public communications for two successful state political campaigns; served as the chief information officer for the New Mexico Office of the Attorney General; migrated the first government agency to Google Apps; speaks at conferences across the nation about implementing new technology; wrote software to extend Google Apps that serves more than half a million users worldwide; and has published numerous technology articles, including the Google Enterprise blog (*http://googleenterprise.blog spot.com/*).

Colophon

The animal on the cover of *Google Apps Script, 2nd edition* is a Black-throated Blue Warbler (*Setophaga caerulescens*). This common songbird is native to North America, and it prefers areas with large forests or uninterrupted woodland. While the Warbler population in North America is stable and growing, deforestation threatens its winter migratory areas and could eventually have a negative impact on the future of the species.

The German naturalist Johann Friedrich Gmelin first described Black-throated Blue Warblers in 1789; its species name, *caerulescens*, comes from the Latin meaning "turning blue." The male of the species has an inky blue back and head, with a bright white belly and a black throat. Unfortunately, the female is not so colorfully arrayed: she has an olive-brown back and pale yellow underparts.

As a species of songbird, the male Warbler attracts a mate through singing; once a female responds, the two will be monogamous for the breeding season, which runs from May through July. Due to their diet of insects supplemented by berries and seeds, the Warbler builds a nest close to the ground. They prefer woodland that is very dense so that their nests will be better protected from predators by scrub and overgrowth.

After a pair has bonded, the male will often guard the female closely, following her around as she forages for food and collects materials with which to build the nest. Near the end of the mating season, males who were able to create offspring will stay with the nest and sing a special post-breeding song; those that could not find a mate abandon their areas. This behavior allows the males to demonstrate their success and helps females keep track of good nesting and breeding habitats.

The cover image is from Wood's *Animate Creation*. The cover fonts are URW Typewriter and Guardian Sans. The text font is Adobe Minion Pro; the heading font is Adobe Myriad Condensed; and the code font is Dalton Maag's Ubuntu Mono.

Get even more for your money.

Join the O'Reilly Community, and register the O'Reilly books you own. It's free, and you'll get:

- $4.99 ebook upgrade offer
- 40% upgrade offer on O'Reilly print books
- Membership discounts on books and events
- Free lifetime updates to ebooks and videos
- Multiple ebook formats, DRM FREE
- Participation in the O'Reilly community
- Newsletters
- Account management
- 100% Satisfaction Guarantee

Signing up is easy:

1. Go to: oreilly.com/go/register
2. Create an O'Reilly login.
3. Provide your address.
4. Register your books.

Note: English-language books only

To order books online:
oreilly.com/store

For questions about products or an order:
orders@oreilly.com

To sign up to get topic-specific email announcements and/or news about upcoming books, conferences, special offers, and new technologies:
elists@oreilly.com

For technical questions about book content:
booktech@oreilly.com

To submit new book proposals to our editors:
proposals@oreilly.com

O'Reilly books are available in multiple DRM-free ebook formats. For more information:
oreilly.com/ebooks

O'REILLY®

Have it your way.

CPSIA information can be obtained at www.ICGtesting.com
Printed in the USA
LVOW03s1923270314

379214LV00031B/204/P